CONTENTS

P 70

INTRODUCTION

What is *Blueprints: Science*?

Blueprints: Science is a practical teachers' resource specifically written to fulfil all the requirements of the National Curriculum in science for primary schools. It is intended for all teachers, particularly non-science specialists, and provides comprehensive coverage in an easy-to-follow format. *Blueprints: Science* is a rich resource of practical ideas to use alongside other materials within your scheme of work. It gives children meaningful, relevant things to do. *Blueprints: Science Key Stage 1* provides activities for 5–7-year-olds. *Blueprints: Science Key Stage 2* includes activities for 7–11-year-olds. For each Key Stage there is a Teacher's Resource Book and a book of Pupils' Copymasters.

Blueprints and the National Curriculum

This second edition of *Blueprints: Science* closely follows the revised publication *Science in the National Curriculum* (HMSO, 1991). The Teacher's Resource Book is structured around the four Attainment Targets. The Pupils' Copymasters reinforce and extend the activities in this book and also provide materials for teacher-based assessment for use alongside SATs.

Blueprints and topics

Blueprints: Science is a flexible resource and can be used in subject lessons devoted exclusively to the learning of science or in the learning of scientific principles while doing topic work. On page viii of this Teacher's Resource Book is a Topic Planner chart which lists many of the topics in common use. Alongside each topic title is an indicator to show at which Levels and in which Attainment Targets (ATs) there is work which can easily make a contribution to the topic.

Blueprints: Science Key Stage 2

This Teacher's Resource Book provides dozens of practical explorations and activities through Key Stage 2. The book is arranged in four sections. The sections relate to work expected of children through this Key Stage, i.e. ATs 1–4 at Levels 2, 3, 4 and 5. Within each section the heading for work in each Attainment Target is a reproduced extract from the Statutory Provisions, comprising the AT title and applicable Statements of Attainment with examples. A sample extract is given opposite.

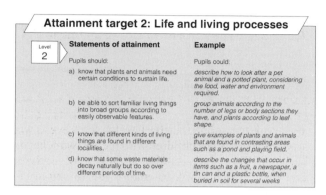

In addition, at the front of each AT section, you will find a reproduction of the relevant programme of study, cross-referenced to the activities for that AT:

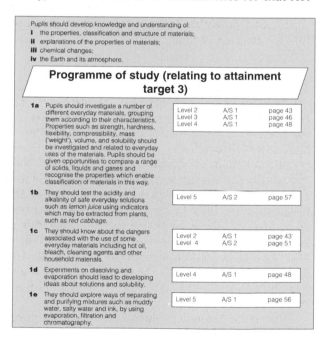

You will find a similar cross-reference on the area of study heading, showing how its activities meet the programme of study:

Area of study 1 | P of S 1b — LIFE-SUSTAINING CONDITIONS — C3

This cross-referencing means that you can work from either the Programme of Study, or the Statement of Attainment, to suit your own needs. You will find the general introduction to the programme of study on page xi.

There are two record sheets at the back, on which you can identify ATs you and the children have worked on, and also note work done which has contributed to AT1.

The Pupils' Copymaster Book provides 115 photo-copiable worksheets linked to many of the activities in this Teacher's Resource Book. The worksheets give the children a chance to record activities and results in an organised way, and in some cases to consolidate learning that has gone before. When completed, the worksheets can be added to children's workfiles or used as exemplar material in pupil profiles. They may also be seen as a resource for teacher assessment. There are two record sheets at the back, on which you can note the copymasters the children have made use of, and their experience of work contributing to AT1.

Attainment Targets 2–4

Across all these ATs *Blueprints: Science Key Stage 2* provides coverage of Levels 2–5. It is expected that most children should master Level 4, but Level 5 work is provided for those children who require work beyond Level 4. There are similar numbers of activities available at each Level, to enable you to employ the Teacher's Resource Book as flexibly as you wish, using earlier activities for revision and consolidation, and later ones for extension.

The Pupils' Copymasters are provided where we felt they would be most appropriate for work on these ATs, as support for busy teachers and to provide frameworks for children's recording.

Attainment Target 1

Attainment Target 1, 'Scientific investigation', has been treated differently from the other ATs. It comprises half the science curriculum at Key Stage 2, and is about 'becoming a scientist', i.e. it concentrates on the methods of scientific enquiry, rather than substantive knowledge. In the section for AT1 there is a discussion of how children can work to meet the programme of study for this AT. We have, however, chosen to use the activities in all the other ATs as vehicles for the acquisition of AT1 skills. Symbols have been created to denote coverage of these skills and these are used throughout the rest of the book and in the copymasters to show how and where AT1 skills are being covered.

Information technology skills are the only exception. Activities related to these appear under AT1.

Record keeping

There are two photocopiable record sheets at the back of the Teacher's Resource Book and the Pupils' Copymasters Book. We suggest you use these as follows.

Teacher's Resource Record Sheet 1: Photocopy one per child and record how many experiences relating to each aspect of AT1 each child has had. This is a matter for your own judgement. Some activities enable work on many aspects of AT1, others few. The kinds of enquiry the children can undertake will depend also on how you set up the activities. A completed sheet 1 may look like the following.

Sheet 2: Photocopy one per child and record which ATs the children have worked at. There are three columns which you can shade in or put a tick in. They can be labelled thus:

a introduced to . . .
b has difficulty/needs more work on . . .
c understood . . .

A completed sheet 2 may look like this:

RECORD SHEET 1: AT1 — Key Stage Two

RECORD SHEET 2: ATs 2–4 — Key Stage Two

Pupils' Copymaster Record Sheet 1: Photocopy one per child and put a tick against those aspects of AT1 which, in your judgement, the child has experienced in work they have recorded on the copymasters. There is a bar code containing the symbols we consider appropriate at the top of each copymaster to help you.

Sheet 2: Photocopy one per child and list the copymasters each child has worked on. The three columns could be used as suggested above, that is:

a introduced to...
b has difficulty/needs more work on...
c understood...

HOW TO USE THIS BOOK

If you have only the Teacher's Resource Book
You can use this book as a flexible resource which you can consult for ideas, activities and investigations to work on with children.

To use in class:

1 Consult the appropriate part of the Programme of Study reprinted at the start of each AT.

2 Consider, in the light of the Programme of Study and your school records, the Levels at which the children are working.

3 Consult the appropriate parts of the section on AT1.

4 Within the chosen Levels of the ATs, look at the Areas of Study and choose those that will fit in with your work plans for the children.

5 Within the chosen Areas of Study select activities which best fit your management plans and resourcing.

6 Assemble the equipment which you and the children need to carry out the activities.

7 As each activity is completed use Record Sheets 1 and 2 to record what the children have done.

If you also have the Pupils' Copymasters
8 Identify the appropriate copymasters and ensure that you have enough copies. There are notes on how to use the sheets in this book. You will find the appropriate sheets referred to in this book with this symbol:

Give them to the children at the optimal time for them to do the necessary recording.

9 Use Record Sheets 1 and 2 to record what the children have done on the copymasters.

TOPIC PLANNER

If you wish to include science in your topic work, look down the following list of 20 common topic titles and identify any that are close to the topic that you are planning. Alongside the title we have indicated, by Attainment Target, the location of activities in this book which support that topic. Depending on the emphasis within the work you are planning, you may be able to incorporate activities in ATs and at Levels other than those we have drawn attention to.

Topic Title	Levels	Attainment Targets			Related Topics
		2	3	4	
Families	2	●			Animals Change Health
	3	●			
	4	●			
	5	●			
Animals	2	●			Families Food Underground Seasons Health
	3	●			
	4	●			
	5	●			
Food, Nutrition and the Environment	2	●			Animals Weather Water Seasons Health
	3	●			
	4	●			
	5	●			
Weather	2				Food Water Buildings Seasons Space
	3				
	4		●		
	5		●	●	
Water	2	●	●		Food Weather
	3	●	●		
	4		●		
	5		●		

viii

Topic Title	Levels	Attainment Targets			Related Topics
		2	3	4	
Transport	2		●	●	Communications Industrial Revolution
	3		●	●	
	4		●	●	
	5			●	
Underground	2	●			Animals What is it Made of?
	3	●			
	4	●			
	5	●			
Buildings	2			●	Weather Change Our School Our Village/Town Industrial Revolution What is it Made of?
	3				
	4			●	
	5			●	
Time	2				Buildings Seasons Communications Change Industrial Revolution
	3			●	
	4			●	
	5			●	
Seasons	2	●		●	Animals Food Weather Time Change Our School Our Village/Town
	3	●		●	
	4	●		●	
	5			●	
Space	2			●	Weather Change What is it Made of?
	3			●	
	4			●	
	5			●	
Communications	2				Transport Time Industrial Revolution
	3			●	
	4			●	
	5			●	

Topic Title	Levels	Attainment Targets			Related Topics
		2	3	4	
Change	2	●	●		Families Buildings Time Seasons Space
	3	●	●		
	4	●	●		
	5	●	●		
Our School	2			●	Buildings Seasons
	3				
	4			●	
	5				
Our Village/ Town	2			●	Buildings Seasons
	3	●			
	4	●		●	
	5	●			
The Industrial Revolution	2		●		Transport Buildings Time Communications
	3		●		
	4		●		
	5				
What is it Made of?	2		●		Underground Buildings Space
	3		●		
	4		●		
	5		●		
Safety First	2	●	●		Health
	3				
	4	●	●		
	5				
Health/ Feeling ill	2	●			Families Animals Food Safety
	3				
	4	●			
	5				

Topic Title	Levels	Attainment Targets			Related Topics
		2	3	4	
The Annual Trip; castle, safari park, museum, etc.	2	Can cover all ATs and be related to most other topics, depending on where you go!			
	3				
	4				
	5				

Programme of study: Supports attainment targets 1–4; levels 2–5

General introduction

To communicate, to relate science to everyday life and to explore, are essential elements of a developing experience of science.

Communication: pupils should have opportunities to continue to develop and use communication skills in presenting their ideas and in reporting their work to audiences, including pupils, teachers, parents and other adults. In giving an account, orally or in writing, they should be encouraged to present information in an ordered manner. They should be introduced to the conventions used in diagrams, tables, charts, graphs, symbols and models. Pupils should be given opportunities to participate in small-group discussions and should be introduced to books, charts and other sources from which they can gain information. Pupils should use computers to store, retrieve and present their work and extend their understanding of information transfer.

Science in everyday life: as pupils begin to gain increasing knowledge and understanding, they should be given the opportunity to develop further an awareness of the role and importance of science in everyday life including personal health and safety and the use of microelectronic devices to control appliances in the home. This awareness might be developed through investigations, case studies, secondary sources of information, and visits. Industrial contexts should be introduced, alongside those of domestic and environmental contexts, as starting points for pupils' work in science.

ATTAINMENT TARGET 1: Scientific investigation

Pupils should develop the intellectual and practical skills which will allow them to explore and investigate the world of science and develop a fuller understanding of scientific phenomena, the nature of the theories explaining these, and the procedures of scientific investigation. This should take place through activities that require a progressively more systematic and quantified approach which develops and draws upon an increasing knowledge and understanding of science. The activities should encourage the ability to plan and carry out investigations in which pupils:

i   ask questions, predict and hypothesise;

ii observe, measure and manipulate variables;

iii interpret their results and evaluate scientific evidence.

Programme of study (relating to attainment target 1)

Programme of study

Pupils should be encouraged to develop investigative skills and understanding of science through activities which:

- help them to use and develop scientific knowledge and understanding;
- encourage the raising and answering of questions;
- foster understanding and practice of safety and care;
- are within their everyday experience and provide opportunities to explore, with increasing precision;
- build on existing practical skills;
- require an increasingly systematic approach involving the identification and manipulation of key variables;
- involve the use of secondary sources as well as first-hand observations;
- include the use of computers and simple electronic devices, such as digital watches, in their experimental work.

These activities should:

- involve variables to be controlled in the development of 'fair tests';
- involve problems which can be solved qualitatively, but which increasingly allow for some quantification of the variables.

Statements of attainment

Pupils should carry out investigation in which they:

Level 2

a) ask questions such as 'how...?' 'why...?' and 'what will happen if...?', suggest ideas and make predictions.

b) make a series of related observations.

c) use their observations to support conclusions and compare what they have observed with what they expected.

Level 3

a) suggest questions, ideas and predictions, based on everyday experience, which can be tested.

b) observe closely and quantify by measuring using appropriate instruments.

c) recognise that their conclusions may not be valid unless a fair test has been carried out.

d) distinguish between a description of what they observed and a simple explanation of how and why it happened.

Examples

Pupils could:

ask why toy cars go further on a smooth surface than on a rough surface? They could suggest that on very smooth surfaces cars will go faster and further but on a very rough surface they will hardly move at all.

mark the distance a car travels along different surfaces.

explain that 'My car went furthest on the hall floor. This is what I thought. Rough carpet slows cars down.'

suggest what is needed to help cress to grow, how these ideas might be tested and what might happen.

measure the growth of the cress seedlings over a period of time using a ruler.

show that they understand that the different batches of seeds should be planted at the same time, in similar containers and given the same amount of water.

come to a generalised statement such as 'this box of cress grew more than the one kept in the dark; this is because cress needs light to grow'.

Programme of study	Statements of attainment	Examples
• encourage the formulation of testable hypotheses, drawing on their developing knowledge and understanding;	Pupils should:	Pupils could:

Level 4

Programme of study	Statements of attainment	Examples
• develop skills of using equipment and measurement, encouraging them to make decisions about when, what and how to measure;	a) ask questions, suggest ideas and make predictions, based on some relevant prior knowledge, in a form which can be investigated.	*be asked to investigate how best to keep a container of water hot. Children could suggest using insulating material and predict that a thicker layer of a material is better than a thin one.*
• encourage systematic listing and recording of data, for example, in *frequency tables and bar charts*;	b) carry out a fair test in which they select and use appropriate instruments to measure quantities such as volume and temperature.	*identify variables which affect the rate at which water cools. They could identify temperature as the variable to be measured, the thickness of material as the variable to be changed, and keep the other variables (amount of water, starting temperature, type of insulation, type of container) the same. They could choose appropriate instruments to measure quantities such as the volume of water used, water temperature and cooling time.*
• promote the search for patterns in data;		
• foster the interpretation of data, and evaluation against the demands of the problem;		
• involve the capture, transmission, storage and retrieval of information using computers and sensors;		
• encourage pupils to appraise their investigations and suggest improvements to their methods.	c) draw conclusions which link patterns in observations or results to the original question, prediction or idea.	*explain that thicker materials are better insulators. 'With the thick materials the temperature fell by 13°C but with the thin it fell by 22°C.'*

Level 5

	Statements of attainment	Examples
	a) formulate hypotheses where the causal link is based on scientific knowledge, understanding or theory.	*consider the factors that affect the rate at which bread dough rises and suggest that the temperature might be important. They could decide to test the raising of some dough at temperatures within the range at which living organisms normally survive.*
	b) choose the range of each of the variables involved to produce meaningful results.	*select temperatures between room temperature and 60°C in order to obtain measurable changes in the time available and suggest other variables to be controlled, such as the shape of the container and the amounts of yeast, sugar, flour and water.*
	c) evaluate the validity of their conclusions by considering different interpretations of their experimental evidence.	*consider different explanations for the faster rising of the dough at warmer temperatures, such as the yeast producing more carbon dioxide or the gas bubbles expanding as they get hotter. They could recognise that the former is the more likely explanation for the differences observed.*

Notes on the Programme of Study for AT1

The Programme of Study, as set out on pp. 1–2, comprises two lists. In our view the first sets out how teachers can help children become scientists. They are the criteria against which you can decide whether to include an Activity in your working timetable.

The second list is all about scientific method: those investigative skills that all scientists use. In summary form they comprise the following: 'fair tests', quantifying variables, formulating hypotheses; using measuring equipment; systematic recording, searching for patterns and interpretation and evaluation of data; using IT; appraisal and improvement.

Below is a commentary on each of the skills in turn. You may choose to meet these skill requirements by either:

● doing activities planned with skill acquistion as the objective, or

● doing substantive activities where, aside from the knowledge they gain, children can be introduced to or practise skills. (To help with this we have already identified AT1 skills in use when the children have done work on a copymaster and the AT1 logos label them.)

'Fair tests'

The concept of a 'fair test' is central to scientific method. Controlling variables and making objective comparisons is the way in which scientists work. Children need to understand that science relies on measurable comparisons which are not altered by prejudice, luck or inaccurate work. A 'fair test' has these characteristics:

● Control of variables
● A series of observations
● Stated accuracy of observation/measurement.

Quantifying variables

We carry out experiments to see what happens when things in our world change. Factors that have to do with the changes are called variables. Children need to begin their learning by identifying salient variables. They should, with experience, become skilled at suggesting ways these might be controlled and measured.

Formulating testable hypotheses

Unlike our day-to-day problem-solving, which does not have to be systematic, scientific method requires that we continually attempt to confirm or discredit our theories by putting forward new ideas that can be tested out both by us and other people. Children can be helped to think of ideas that conform to these rules.

Using measuring equipment

Scientific method has rigorous rules about how ideas should be set out and tested. There are also rules about the appropriate use of equipment. Children need to know about working safely, taking care of equipment, choosing equipment which is appropriate for the kind of task in hand and taking measurements carefully. The range is from measuring jugs, rulers and spring balances to electronic sensors and microscopes. The kinds of decisions appropriate for the children are these:

● What can we measure?
● How best can it be measured?
● How many measurements do we need?
● How accurate are my measurements?

Listing and recording data

It is part of scientific method to be patient and painstaking in collecting data and thorough, scrupulous and systematic in recording, organising and presenting

it. Through guided practice from simple lists through to charts and tables children should be helped to make decisions about how they set about putting data on paper or the computer. The National Curriculum Statutory Orders for Mathematics AT1 are also helpful in establishing data organising skills in children. Consult them to find ways of linking skills in maths and science.

Data patterns

Successful and systematic collection and recording of data make it possible to look for pattern. A pattern of data is essential for us to pose an explanation for what happens in an experiment. Even chance discovery in the history of science has depended on a search for data pattern. Give the children plenty of practice in looking for pattern in their own results and those of their classmates. Do tell the children that the pattern we look for may demonstrate a positive *or* a negative *or* no link between variables, and all these patterns can be equally important.

Data interpretation and evaluation

This links closely to an understanding of data pattern. However, it may be set separately in the Programme of Study in order to draw our attention to the 'feedback' ideas in experimentation. When they have done an experiment children need to be able to say 'What do my results mean when I recall what it is I was trying to do?' This promotes judgements about the success of the experiment and how it could be modified. The National Curriculum Statutory Orders for Technology (especially ATs 1 and 4) stress the importance of these kinds of skills.

Information technology

A wide range of computing and sensing equipment is now available in schools, ranging from calculators to computers, and tape-recorders to electronic sensors. Because experience in handling information using technology can be episodic in school, we feel it is a skill area in which teachers may want to plan extra activities giving skill practice. We have set out some suggested activities under the heading 'Information Technology Skills' below.

Appraisal and improvement

It is by this means that scientists improve on past experiment, produce more valid experimental designs, and carry forward the refinement of theories. It can be difficult to give children more than just a 'flavour' of this process in a busy school year, for there are pressures on you, the teacher, and on the children to cover much curriculum ground. However, with judicious planning, and giving children individual and small-group problem-solving exercises, they should be able to carry some investigations beyond the 'one try and write it up' format of much junior science.

Attainment Target 1

As explained in the introduction, all the skills required for AT1 are developed through the activities in ATs

2– 4. In order to enable you to identify the work on scientific investigations as the children work on the content of science in ATs 2–4, the complete average of AT1 has been summarised by a set of symbols. You will find these symbols used at the end of appropriate activities to denote which AT1 skills are covered, and on the accompanying copymasters. You can record children's experience of AT1 skills on the record sheet at the back of the book.

The content of AT1 at each level is summarised by the following symbols:

Level 2

Ask questions Identify Measure List Record findings Interpret findings

Level 3

Formulate hypotheses Identify Fair/ unfair test Use instruments Quantify variables

Record Interpret charts Interpret & generalise Sequencing

Level 4

Raise questions for investigation Formulate hypotheses Construct fair tests Identify and control variables Select and use instruments Quantify variables

Follow instructions and diagrams Do it safely Record Draw tables, charts and graphs Draw conclusions Prose description

Level 5

Investigation, selection and design Identify and manipulate variables Select and use instruments Quantify variables Statement of data patterns

Information Technology skills

Here is a mixed bag of suggested activities for children to do. They are not tied to Levels, and the sooner children can master the skills involved, the more adept they will become at doing experiments scientifically.

SENDING MESSAGES

Purpose
To demonstrate that messages can be transmitted in a number of ways.

Materials needed
Second timers, information about heraldry, badges and flags.

Activity 1: Messages using human body and voice
Take the children into the playground. Let each of them find a partner. Then tell the whole group that they are going to try a number of ways of getting a message to their friend. Let each pair label themselves A and B. Get the Bs to stand in a line on the far side of the playground. Brief the As that they are to stay in a line opposite their partner and give them a message firstly by running to whisper it in their ear. Then get them to shout it, and finally let them signal it across the playground. Reverse the As and Bs so that everyone has a turn at message-taking. Discuss which method seemed the most efficient and why.

Divide the children into an even number of small groups with about four children in each group. Give each group a 'name', e.g. a colour or a letter. Pair off the groups so that each is working with another group. Let one group of each pair stand at one side of the playground with their partner group on the opposite side. Let one group of each pair confer to decide how they will deliver a message to their partner group. As you give them a message, get them to start the timer. See how long it takes and whether this method allows accurate delivery.

Activity 2: Codes
Discuss simple codes for messages. The children will have some ideas from their attempts at signalling in Activity 1. Let the children invent codes based on colours, shapes and movement, e.g. arm or leg positions. Look at and discuss the codes behind, for example, traffic-lights, heraldry, the school badge and flags flown by ships. The children can have fun encoding and decoding messages. Their codes can be written up in book form and displayed.

Activity 3: Sending long-distance messages
Look at the everyday ways of sending messages over a long distance, including letters, telephone calls and television. Arrange to exchange letters with a similar class in another school. Discuss the way we set up the message, how we pay for delivery and the route the message takes. Work out the time between posting and delivery.

Discuss the advantages and disadvantages of making a telephone call, compared with sending a letter.

Talk about the two-way possibilities in letters and telephone calls and compare with television messages which are one-way.

Use copymaster 1 for the children to record the routes taken by a letter and a telephone message.

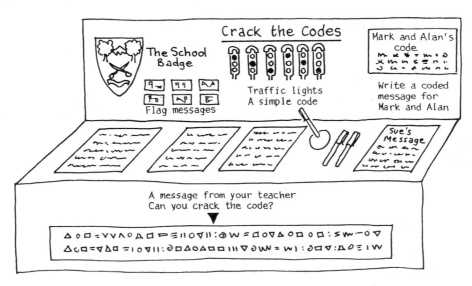

INFORMATION STORAGE

Purpose
To show that information can be stored in a variety of ways.

Materials needed
Access to school library; telephone directories, used envelopes addressed to the children's families; maps.

Activity 1: School library

Look round the school library with the children. Ask them to try to find out how it is arranged. Are the books arranged alphabetically, by author, by topic, subject or size? Then discuss how you find the information you are looking for. Give the children some puzzle questions to see if they can 'access the information store' (i.e. look up the answers).

Activity 2: Telephone directories

Show the children what is contained in a directory. Let them look up their own telephone number, that of a friend, the police station, library and others. Show the children what local codes are, and what national and international codes look like.

Activity 3: Post-codes

Get the children to bring in a used envelope addressed to their family, with the post-code on it. Using a map of the locality, and post-code information found in some telephone directories, plot the location of post-codes, and discuss what information is therefore 'stored' in a post-code.

Activity 4: Maps

Let the children study a map key, identify some of the symbols and seek them out on the map. The map is an information 'store'.

ELECTRONIC STORAGE OF INFORMATION

Purpose

To show that electronic devices can be used to store information, and to access some information.

Materials needed

Tape recorders with cassettes, photo albums or folders, digital watches, calculators, video cameras with film and playback machine, computer and software, packages with bar codes on them, access to a telephone.

Activity 1: Using tape recorders

Show the children how to load a cassette, make a recording and replay it. Let the children work in pairs, making tape recordings of each other, sound effects and interviews. When they are skilled at producing a good recording, let them decide on a topic of current interest, or where a tape recording is an asset. They can then create a written/audio record of their topic, and they can present it in a photo album or folder.

Activity 2: Tape recorders: sound effects

Let the children record sound effects around the school, e.g. footsteps, creaking doors, rain on the roof, a running tap, and then use these sounds as a resource for drama lessons.

Activity 3: Digital watches

Let the children use a digital watch and set a time-limit to an activity marked by an alarm.

Activity 4: Bar codes

Discuss what these mean and how they are used in supermarkets.

Activity 5: Speaking clock

Let the children ring the speaking clock, and then discuss how it operates. Explain to them that it works on a radio signal from an atomic clock.

Activity 6: Children's use of information stores

Let the children list their own uses of electronic information stores, including the phone with a number memory, pelican crossings, computer games, video-recorders.

*Listen and learn about our projects

Read Kathy's Book

The School Bird Table

Listen to the bird sounds

tape

Project index

A The weather in May
B School neighbours
C Playground project

Project A → TAPE BOOK

Project B → TAPE BOOK

Project C → TAPE BOOK

Activity 7: Calculators

Use electronic calculators to play a variety of number games. Give the children the chance to use memory, memory recall and iteration. (Choose calculators that do not round up automatically and will iterate, i.e. when you key **x + y =** and continue pressing **+**, **y** is repeatedly added on.)

Activity 8: School video

A real store of information that the children will understand can be made by arranging with other staff and your headteacher and class that you film a day in the life of a group of children. The video is part of school archives, as the children will realise when you show it to them after a couple of years.

Activity 9: Videos

Help the children to write scripts and storyboards for a short video about some aspect of their work. Film it and play back. Add to school resources.

Copymaster 2 can be used for a storyboard layout.

Activity 10: Computers

Show the children how to load software and access it themselves.

Let the children play computer games and store their entries or scores.

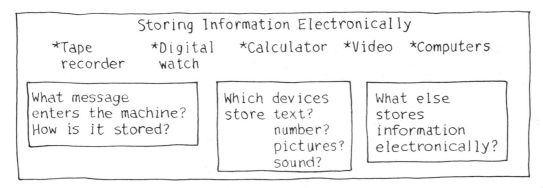

Storing Information Electronically

*Tape recorder *Digital watch *Calculator *Video *Computers

What message enters the machine? How is it stored?

Which devices store text? number? pictures? sound?

What else stores information electronically?

RETRIEVAL OF INFORMATION

Purpose

To be able to retrieve information stored on a computer.

Materials needed

Computer and data base, graphics and sounds software.

Activity 1: Retrieval of text and numbers

Use a commercially produced package, bought with the advice of county advisers, with which children can access information. Give them puzzle questions which they can only answer by accessing the appropriate information. Data bases made by children in the school can also be used.

Activity 2: Creation of and retrieval from data base

Show the children how to create and use a data base to organise information. Either create the data base about the children themselves, or about something that interests them, such as cars, TV personalities, storybook heroes and heroines or space facts. The children should learn how to put the information in and know how to access it in a variety of ways.

Activity 3: Computer graphics

Use a graphics package to show children what can be done on screen. Let them use the package and print out their efforts. Some exciting and comparatively inexpensive art packages are now available.

Activity 4: Computer sound

Use a software package with sound effects, so that children can get computer sound feedback. There are music packages available with which children can play and be creative.

7

Pupils should develop knowledge and understanding of:

i life processes and the organisation of living things;

ii variation and the mechanisms of inheritance and evolution;

iii populations and human influences within ecosystems;

iv energy flows and cycles of matter within ecosystems.

Programme of study (relating to attainment target 2)

1a Pupils should be introduced to the major organs and organ systems of mammals and flowering plants. They should explore some aspects of feeding, support, movement and behaviour in relation to themselves and other animals. They should explore ideas about the processes of breathing, circulation, growth and reproduction.

Level 2	A/S 2	page 10
Level 2	A/S 3	page 11
Level 3	A/S 1	page 18
Level 3	A/S 2	page 20
Level 4	A/S 1	page 27
Level 5	A/S 1	page 37
Level 5	A/S 2	page 38

1b They should investigate the factors that affect plant growth, for example, *light intensity, temperature, and amount of water.*

Level 2	A/S 1	page 10
Level 3	A/S 10	page 25

1c They should study how microbes and lifestyle can affect health, and learn about factors that contribute to good health including the defence systems of the body; diet, personal hygiene, safe handling of food, dental care and exercise. They should be introduced to the fact that while all medicines are drugs, not all drugs are medicines. They should begin to be aware of the harmful effect on health resulting from an abuse of tobacco, alcohol and other drugs.

Level 2	A/S 4	page 12
Level 4	A/S 2	page 28

2a Pupils should investigate and measure the similarities and differences between themselves, animals and plants and fossils. They should be introduced to how plants and animals can be preserved as fossils.

Level 2	A/S 5	page 14
Level 2	A/S 6	page 15
Level 4	A/S 3	page 30
Level 4	A/S 5	page 30
Level 4	A/S 6	page 31
Level 4	A/S 10	page 34
Level 5	A/S 3	page 39

2b They should have the opportunity to develop skills in identifying locally occurring species of animals and plants by observing structural features and making and using simple keys.

Level 2	A/S 5	page 14
Level 4	A/S 3	page 29

2c They should be introduced to the idea that information is passed from one generation to the next.

| Level 3 | A/S 3 | page 20 |
| Level 5 | A/S 3 | page 39 |

3a Pupils should explore and investigate at least two different habitats and the animals and plants that live there. They should find out how animals and plants are suited to these habitats and how they are influenced by environmental conditions including seasonal and daily changes and measure these changes using a variety of instruments. They should develop an awareness and understanding of the necessity for sensitive collection and care of living things used as the subject of any study of the environment.

Level 2	A/S 7	page 16
Level 3	A/S 4	page 21
Level 4	A/S 7	page 31
Level 4	A/S 8	page 32

3b They should study aspects of the local environment affected by human activity, for example, *farming, industry, mining or quarrying* and consider the benefits and detrimental effects of these activities.

| Level 3 | A/S 5 | page 22 |

3c They should be made aware of the competition between living things and their need for food, shelter and a place to reproduce.

| Level 4 | A/S 9 | page 33 |

3d They should study the effects of pollution on the survival of living things.

Level 3	A/S 6	page 23
Level 3	A/S 7	page 23
Level 3	A/S 8	page 24
Level 3	A/S 9	page 25
Level 5	A/S 4	page 40
Level 5	A/S 5	page 40

4a Pupils should be introduced to the idea that green plants use energy from the Sun to produce food and that food chains are a way of representing feeding relationships.

| Level 4 | A/S 11 | page 36 |

4b They should investigate the key factors in the process of decay such as temperature, moisture, air and the role of microbes. They should build on their investigations of decay and consider the significant features of waste disposal procedures, for example in *sewage disposal and composting*, and the usefulness of any products.

Level 2	A/S 8	page 17
Level 2	A/S 9	page 18
Level 5	A/S 6	page 41

Attainment target 2: Life and living processes

<table>
<tr><td>Level
2</td><td colspan="2"></td></tr>
</table>

Statements of attainment	**Example**
Pupils should:	Pupils could:
a) know that plants and animals need certain conditions to sustain life.	*describe how to look after a pet animal and a potted plant, considering the food, water and environment required.*
b) be able to sort familiar living things into broad groups according to easily observable features.	*group animals according to the number of legs or body sections they have, and plants according to leaf shape.*
c) know that different kinds of living things are found in different localities.	*give examples of plants and animals that are found in contrasting areas such as a pond and playing field.*
d) know that some waste materials decay naturally but do so over different periods of time.	*describe the changes that occur in items such as a fruit, a newspaper, a tin can and a plastic bottle, when buried in soil for several weeks.*

 Area of study 1 | P of S 1b

LIFE-SUSTAINING CONDITIONS

C3

Purpose
To show that plants can only thrive when their vital needs are met.

Materials needed
Seeds, small flowerpots, seed compost, small watering can or jug, sugar paper.

Activity 1: Plant needs
Help the children to decide what they think a plant needs to grow. Then help them test some of these ideas by growing grass, cress or broad beans under the following conditions:

Pot 1: soil, no water, light. Plant the seed. Do not water. Place in light.
Pot 2: soil, water, no light. Plant the seed. Water regularly but keep covered.
Pot 3: no soil, water, light. Put seed in empty pot. Water regularly and place in the light.
Pot 4: soil, water, light. Plant the seed. Water regularly and place in the light.

Pot 2 can be placed in the dark by making a cylinder out of sugar paper to enclose the pot, and fitting it with a lid. Depending on the kind of seed and other environmental conditions the seeds may all germinate, but the growth should be most vigorous where all the experimental needs are met, i.e. pot 4.

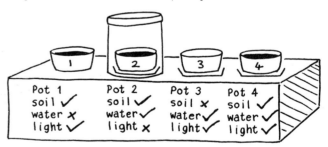

The children can record the results of the experiment on copymaster 3.

 Area of study 2 | P of S 1a

HUMAN NEEDS

C4

Purpose
To help the children examine what their basic needs are.

Materials needed
Dolls with doll-size furniture, clothes and crockery; or doll's house or model farm.

10

Activity 1: Our needs

Discuss with the children what they think their needs are, using the dolls or the house/farm to demonstrate all the things we do every day to satisfy basic needs. The need for warmth, food and drink, air and sleep will come out of the discussion.

The children can then help set up a display of dolls to show life-sustaining needs. Or they could set up the doll's house/farm with dolls eating, sleeping, dressed in clothes and outside getting 'fresh air'.

You can explain to the children that we have other needs that may not be *essential* to life, but which are nonetheless very important. They include love and exercise.

Get the children to record in pictures their own needs on copymaster 4.

Area of study 3	P of S 1a	# LOOKING AFTER OTHER ANIMALS

Purpose
To learn how pets and other animals should be looked after.

Materials needed
A range of pets; beginners' books about pets.

Activity 1: Pets
Do a 'pet survey' among the children. Get the group of children with each pet to record how they care for their

pets, and display as a mini-topic. Those children who do not have a pet can learn about the school pet if there is one, or work on a pet belonging to one of their friends.

Activity 2: Animal care
Invite someone to come and talk to the children about animal care. It could be a zookeeper, petshop owner or someone representing the RSPCA or RSPB. Alternatively, consult the local 'what's on' section in

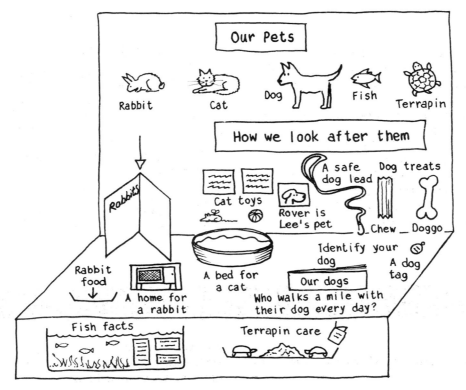

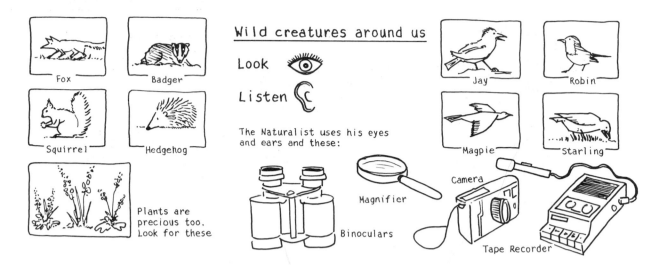

the paper or library to find out whether there is a local Natural History Group or Ornithological Society. Such a group may welcome the chance to tell children how to protect the habitat of wild creatures and how to observe them properly. If you do decide to invite a visitor, the visit does require some research on your part. If possible, meet the speaker, establish what he/she needs (e.g. projector, birdcage) and give him/her a brief. Tell him/her the context for the children's learning and the kind of thing you would like to be included in the talk, if possible. Try and persuade him/her to bring some slides (or preferably live creatures) for the children to see. Also ask if there are some things which he/she can bring that you may borrow for a while. For example, a bag of birdseed, a brush used for cleaning an elephant or even an unused dog kennel from the pet shop will contribute much more to the children's learning than any number of slides. You will also have the makings of an enthralling display.

Activity 3: Pet show

Have a pets' corner or pet show. You will need some parental help and the permission of the parents. Give the children a written note to say that they are allowed to bring their pet to school on the special day, providing it is in a container through which it can be seen and from which it cannot escape. Cover everywhere with newspaper and be prepared to spend the day being a zookeeper. The children who bring pets can be the experts on pet care. All the children can do some close observation and some drawing from life, and make comparisons of the needs of different pets. You may get the chance to compile a short quiz on the show, with questions such as: 'What do rabbits eat?', 'What does Monica give her hamster to play with?'; and tasks such as: 'Name one nocturnal pet', 'Name one pet which eats all kinds of food', etc.

| Area of study 4 | P of S 1c | **LOOKING AFTER YOURSELF** | C5 |

Purpose
To persuade children to do certain important things for their health and safety.

Materials needed
A wash bag and contents; empty food packages from all the main food groups; trainers and PE kit along with, for example, a skipping-rope and ball; a pillow and bedding or a made up doll's bed. Booklets about road safety (including a road floor mat and toys or local road map). Information about 'stranger danger'. Books about safety in the home, the danger of empty medicine bottles, etc.

Activity 1: Personal hygiene
Discuss cleanliness and examine the contents of the wash bag, which may include soap, flannel, toothbrush and paste. Start a display with these items.

Activity 2: Healthy eating
Talk about the four main food groups: proteins, carbohydrates, fats and vitamins and minerals. Discuss what we should eat every day for health. Mention some of the foods which we should avoid or have only occasionally. Ask the children to bring in the packaging for healthy foods belonging to the four groups and add these to the display started in Activity 1.

Activity 3: Keeping fit
Discuss the importance of exercise to keep healthy and examine the trainers, PE kit and exercise aids (rope, ball) to fuel the discussion, and to get the children talking about appropriate kit for exercise and equipment which helps us to exercise. Add these to the display.

Be clean
soap
washgear

Wash away those bacteria

Eat well
Proteins
Carbohydrates
Fats
Vitamins and minerals

Eat food from each group every day

Exercise
21

Say NO to too much TV

Sleep well

Activity 4: Sleep and rest
Display the bedding or doll's bed, having discussed the importance of rest and sleep.

Activity 5: Staying safe
A project on safety on the roads, 'stranger danger' and staying safe in the home can take weeks to study. If you wish to study it in depth (e.g. because the children seem unaware of the important issues) then try a cross-curricular topic which will meet some of the requirements of other subjects. A road safety project can involve the construction of a road scene on the playmat, or older children could mark the road hazards on a local road map. 'Stranger danger' can be covered with the help of a visit from a police officer.

Safety in the home raises many important points about which children should be informed, including toys left on the floor, electricity, naked flames, hot pans and kettles and medicines. The health and safety display can be extended enormously using all this information. Alternatively, create a separate 'safety at home' display.

Use copymaster 5 for children to picture record.

Safe at home?

Tidy toys

Do not touch electric points

Keep away from fire

Do not go near the cooker

Do not touch

Medicines Do not touch

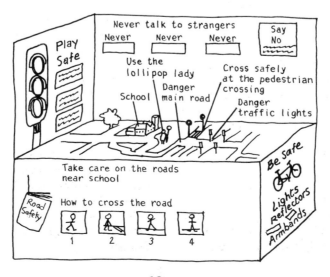

Play Safe

Never talk to strangers
Never   Never   Never

Say No

Use the lollipop lady

School   Danger main road

Cross safely at the pedestrian crossing

Danger traffic lights

Take care on the roads near school

Road Safety

How to cross the road
1   2   3   4

Be Safe
Lights
Reflectors
Armbands

CHARACTERISTICS OF LIVING THINGS

Purpose
To begin to group living creatures according to their characteristics.

Materials needed
Mini-beasts (e.g. spiders, woodlice, caterpillars) and other available animals; bug-bottles and containers to collect animals in and magnifiers, where necessary, to view them.

Activity 1: Animal varieties
Look carefully at a number of living creatures with the children. If you have school pets such as a budgie or fish use them. If there are no school pets, collect mini-beasts. Remember where they were found so that they can be returned. Lift a stone where the soil is damp, shake a bush (having first spread newspaper or a plastic sheet beneath it), upturn a pile of leaves and there should be beetles, ladybirds, woodlice, snails, earthworms and more. Put them into see-through lidded pots. Make sure they are displayed where they are well-lit (but not left to dry out or overheat). Supply magnifiers and some clues as to what to look for to find similarities and differences.

Activity 2: Vertebrates and invertebrates
Construct a wormery. Set it up alongside some woodlice and a display of shells of animals such as cockles, crabs and winkles and also some creatures with an internal skeleton (e.g. a fish).

The children can try a comparison and record their observations on copymaster 6.

Activity 3: Comparing other creatures with ourselves
Ask the children to do a systematic comparison between a mini-beast or fish and themselves. They will need to have the mini-beast/fish to look at. (If you cannot get a live fish, a mackerel or herring from the fishmonger will do.)

Some possible criteria for comparison appear on copymaster 7.

Activity 4: A visit
Visit a zoo, bird sanctuary or aquarium or garden centre with the children, so that they can make some comparisons between different kinds of living things. You will need to research the kinds of creatures or plants you are going to see beforehand, and give the children clues about what to look for.

PEOPLE ARE ALIKE BUT DIFFER

Purpose
To appreciate that some differences between human beings can be easily measured, and to measure some of them.

Materials needed
Sticky shapes, large sheets of paper to make charts, felt-tip markers, pencils, small slips of paper, coloured sugar paper.

Activity 1: Comparing foot sizes
Ask the children to draw round their right foot on coloured sugar paper and then to cut out the shape and write their name on it. They may find it easier to work in pairs, drawing round each other's feet. On a long strip of paper, e.g. wallpaper or lining paper, draw a 'base'-line. Get the children to lay their cut-outs down so that the 'heel' is touching the base-line (see below). The shapes can be set in order by a child or several children while the rest look on. Start with the smallest, leading up to the biggest. Put the chart on display.

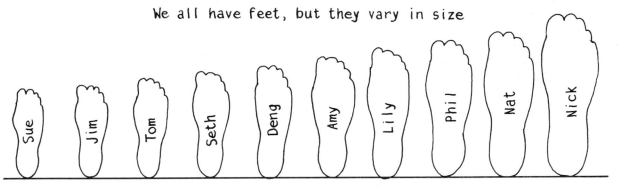

We all have feet, but they vary in size

How many people have feet bigger than Phil?

How many people have feet smaller than Seth?

Activity 2: Comparing height
Fix a strip of paper to the wall or door frame so that the bottom edge just touches the floor. Get each child in turn to stand in their stocking-feet against the strip. Place a stiff piece of card flat on each one's head so that it touches the wall. Make a mark on the strip where the card touches. Then let them step away and write their name by the mark.

children whether they are 'much taller' or 'a bit taller' than one metre. Let them decide whether a metre is a good unit to measure height, or whether we need to have some unit smaller than a metre to measure with. Display the results. If the same children have already done Activity 1 you can look for an association between the data, e.g. people with bigger feet may be taller. There will be opportunities here to talk about similarities in families, e.g. height, hair colour, eye colour, etc. of brothers, sisters, parents and grand-parents.

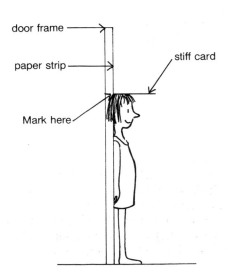

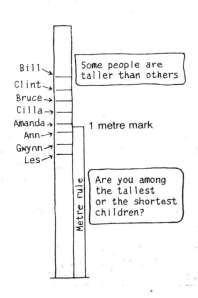

When all the children have a mark on the strip, take a metre rule and mark its height. Discuss with the

15

Activity 3: Comparing handspans

Lay a piece of paper flat on the table and draw a 'start line' down the left-hand side. Ask one child to do the recording. Get each child in turn to place their outstretched hand on the chart, with the starter finger or thumb just touching the 'start line'.

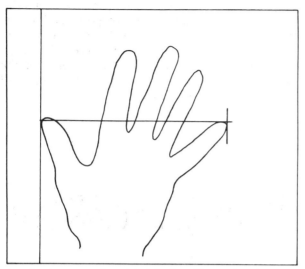

Lay hand on paper in outstretched position and mark beside little finger.

The extent of their handspan can be marked with a pencil, and later marked permanently with a felt tip or sticky paper strip. Put the chart on display.

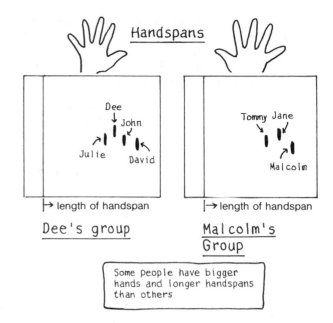

Handspans

length of handspan   length of handspan

Dee's group   Malcolm's Group

Some people have bigger hands and longer handspans than others

Copymaster 8 can be used for the children to make a footsize, height and handspan comparison between themselves and one of their friends.

EXPLORING LOCALITIES

Area of study 7 P of S 3a

Purpose
To look for animals and plants in a variety of localities.

Materials needed
Magnifiers, collecting jars and bags.

Activity 1: The school garden
If your school has a garden, playing field or even a grass verge at the front, let the children explore it to see what they can find in the way of animals that live there, and uncultivated plants that grow there. They may note some of the following:

● What the soil looks like
● Underlying rock (if visible or known)
● Plants and trees (draw and name some of them)
● Birds
● Small creatures like beetles and worms
● Signs of larger animals (droppings or holes)
● Low-growing plants if the grass is cut
● Where it is shady and where in full sun
● Where it is damp and where dry.

The school garden

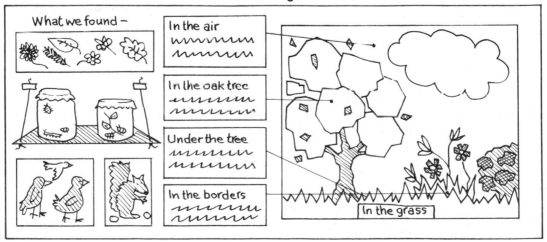

16

The children's findings can be recorded by you at the time using a tape recorder, or you can return to the classroom for a feedback discussion. If you and the children bring sample creatures into the classroom, remember to return them to the spot where found, after you have had a good look at them. Ask the children to produce either a single picture with about four of the things they saw on it, or small pictures which can be added to a collaborative collage. Names and labels can then be added by you.

It may be that yours is an inner-city school with only a tarmac playground. It is still worth looking around the fence yourself to see if there are small creatures under stones, spiders using the fence for their webs, and grass tufts housing other small creatures. If you find 'pockets' housing mini-beasts the children can be introduced to them.

Activity 3: Local parks and gardens
Visit a local park or ask a local resident who has a garden if you may visit. As in Activity 1, let the children look for, draw and name some of the plants and animals they see there. Remind the children that parks and gardens (including the school garden) are worked on by people, and are not entirely 'natural habitats'. This means, for example, that compost dug into the school garden may attract creatures additional to those normally found there. Use this kind of information to show the children that humans have an effect on the environment. Take some photographs to form part of the children's record of their visit.

| Area of study 8 | P of S 4b | **DECAY OF WASTE PRODUCTS** | C9 |

Purpose
To show that some waste decays, but this takes time.

Materials needed
A see-through plastic bag containing some of the kinds of things we put on compost heaps, such as apple cores, potato peelings and tea-leaves; a bucket of 'mature' compost; fallen leaves, leaf-mould and fallen branches which have been on the ground some time.

NB Try to avoid putting these things in the dustbin when you have finished with them. In the interests of the environment they should be returned to the land, and the children should know this too.

Activity 1: Inspection of what is suitable for the compost
To avoid health risks, make a collection of things suitable for composting in a see-through bag and let the children look at the mixture through the bag. You can also cut up an apple and discard the pieces you do not wish to eat into the bag. The children can draw a set of things which will decay on the compost heap.

Copymaster 9 can be used to record that the children can identify what is suitable for the compost.

Activity 2: Inspection of mature compost
Wearing rubber gloves spread some garden compost on a sheet of newspaper. Without touching, the children can inspect the compost and see if they can identify what has gone into it. Tell them the age of the compost and what actually went into it.

Activity 3: Observation of the results of leaf decay
Show the children a collection of fallen leaves and some leaf-mould. Explain that leaf decay takes time. The children can draw a flow chart to show this process, as illustrated here.

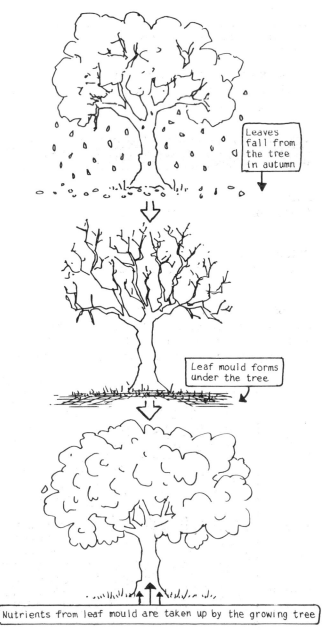

Leaves fall from the tree in autumn

Leaf mould forms under the tree

Nutrients from leaf mould are taken up by the growing tree

Activity 4: Decay in the woods
Take a walk in the woods if you can, and observe what is happening to the fallen leaves and branches. If there are no woods near school collect some partially decayed wood, and display it in class for the children to see and talk about. Then tell the children that you are going to return the wood to the woods from which it came, and do just that.

CLASSIFICATION OF WASTE

Area of study 9 · P of S 4b · C10

Purpose
To identify which kinds of waste can be safely put back into the land and which cannot be disposed of in this way.

Materials needed
Plastic, paper and metal waste samples; a spade and cartons and bottles with a 'green' label, to compare with similar products which lack this label.

Activity 1: Testing what is biodegradable
Bury a piece of plastic bag, a can and a piece of paper in a carefully marked spot in the school garden or in an earthenware flowerpot which is then put outside. Leave it for as long as possible – at least half a term.

Unearth what you have buried and observe and record what has happened.

The experimental results can be recorded pictorially and in writing on copymaster 10.

Activity 2: Packaging: what is biodegradable?
Compare washing-up liquid bottles, washing powder packets and other packaging carrying a biodegradable label with similar packaging which does not. Discuss with the children the responsibility of the manufacturer and consumer in 'choosing green'.

Attainment target 2: Life and living processes

Level 3	Statements of attainment	Examples
	Pupils should:	Pupils could:
	a) know the basic life processes common to humans and other animals.	*identify processes such as feeding, growing, sensing, breathing, moving, and reproducing as common to themselves and familiar animals.*
	b) know that human activity may produce changes in the environment that can affect plants and animals.	*describe a local example of human impact on the environment, such as pollution of a river or the building of a new road.*
	c) know that green plants need light to stay alive and healthy.	*describe what happens to a pot of cress when grown in a dark cupboard compared to a similar pot grown on the window sill.*

THE COMMONALITY OF LIFE PROCESSES

Area of study 1 · P of S 1a · C11, 12

Purpose
To show that feeding, breathing, support, movement and certain behaviours are common to humans and other animals.

Materials needed
Pictures of human beings and other animals, animal skeleton and a model of a human skeleton, shells and fish bones, small live creatures to observe (for example, mini-beasts or school pets), information about the children's pets, books about the animal world, videos of wildlife and pet care programmes.

Activity 1: Feeding
Discuss the kinds of foods that we like to eat. Compare our diet with that of pets like cats and dogs, domestic animals like cows and hens and wild animals including, for example, elephants and lions. Using pictures of a variety of animals, let the children group them according to whether they eat plants (herbivores),

meat (carnivores) or both (omnivores). Discuss the likely effects of an animal's diet on where it lives and how it behaves.

Talk about the effects on animals of a poor diet or insufficient food. Relate this discussion to animal migration and hibernation.

Activity 2: Breathing

Discuss the similarities in breathing between ourselves and other animals. Find out how other animal groups breathe.

Water is the source of oxygen for fish, and the oxygen is taken into their bodies through their gills. The water is sucked in through the mouth and expelled from the gills through the gill covers. Show the children some fish so that they can observe these movements.

Activity 3: Support

Look at an animal skeleton or animal bones or a model of the human skeleton, alongside the shells of creatures like snails and crabs, and the bones of a fish. Talk about how the skeletons of these creatures give support and some protection to their soft organs, as well as a frame on which to attach muscles.

Activity 4: Movement

Watch some wildlife videos and discuss the typical movements of animals in the wild. Look at some fish in water and birds in flight, in life where possible, but also on film or video. With the help of the children assemble all the kinds of words that we can use to describe the movements of fish, birds and other animals.

Ask the children to examine typical movements their pets make, and describe them or draw the movement sequence. Collate all the children's work in a class display.

Use a series of movement lessons to let the children explore the ways of moving typical of a variety of animals. These 'animal movement' routines could form a powerful addition to an assembly or a presentation to other classes.

children in animal masks – ready to move

Our presentation today is about Animal Movement

pictures of animal movement

tape recording of discussion

Activity 5: 'Behaviour'

Discuss with the children the idea that some behaviours are instinctive and some are learned. Instinctive behaviour is common to all members of a species.

Discuss what we mean when we say 'good behaviour' or 'naughty behaviour' in humans; how we communicate with each other, the kinds of 'patterns' in what we do and when certain behaviours are appropriate (for example shaking hands, waving and clapping, having a cuddle). Discuss what non-verbal behaviour is and how, by gesture and expression we, like other animals, can let others know how we feel.

Collect anecdotes about the children's pets. You may need some exploratory questions to start the discussion. Here are some examples:

● What does your dog do when a stranger comes to the door? When he is hungry? When he wants a game?
● What does your hamster do when he first wakes up? When some new food or bedding arrives?

Watch a wildlife video or look at pictures of animals in the wild and talk about how they communicate, how animal 'mums' and 'dads' behave, and what animals do, for example, when sick, content, or frightened. You could add a study of hibernation or migration to the behaviour patterns the children look at.

Activity 6: Life processes

Bring together all the children's work from Activities 1–4 into a whole class consolidation exercise. Here are some examples:

● A dramatic presentation entitled 'The animal world'
● A puppet show about life processes
● The story of Noah with additional discussion about animals' universal requirements.

...children can record some of their observations and discoveries made in the Activities on copymasters 11 and 12.

Area of study 2	P of S 1a	**THE HUMAN LIFE CYCLE**

Purpose
To show what the stages are in a human's life.

Materials needed
Pictures of people, young and old, from magazines; photos brought in by the children of members of their families.

Activity 1: Ages and stages
Discuss ages and stages with the children. Let them order some pictures according to age and stage. Look at generations in their own families with them. Arrange a display of ages and stages using photographs and magazine pictures.

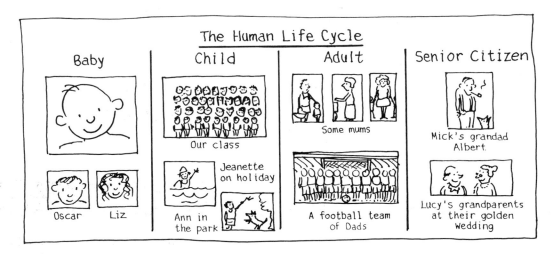

Area of study 3	P of S 2c	**REPRODUCTION**	C13, 14

Purpose
To show that living things reproduce themselves.

Materials needed
Fruits and seeds and parent plants, flowerpots and potting compost; pictures of animal and human families.

Activity 1: Seeds
Let the children carefully examine the seeds and parent plants. If there are trees in or near the school grounds the children can collect their fruits and do rubbings, drawings and observation of them. Cut open a fruit to expose the seed. Talk about what will happen if the seed is planted. Plant some seeds. Get the children to label and care for them. Discuss their growth and when they will be large enough to plant out.

The children can picture record on copymaster 13.

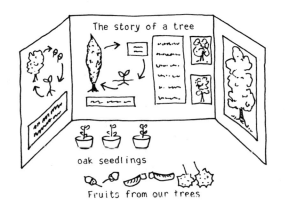

Activity 2: Families
Collect pictures of animal and human families, including photographs brought in by the children. Arrange a family picture exhibition or a large family album containing all these pictures. The children can learn some of the words we use in association with

20

animal families, such as litter, bitch, dog and pups, female, male and offspring. Discuss with them the idea that succeeding generations are always of the same species, in both animals and plants.

Let the children complete copymaster 14 to consolidate this idea.

An album of families

  LIFE PROCESSES: DAYS AND SEASONS

Area of study **4** | P of S **3a** | C15, 16

Purpose
To demonstrate that all living creatures, including plants and animals, are affected by daily and seasonal changes.

Materials needed
Trees in the school grounds or within sight of the school; school pets or the children's own pets for observation; reference books on plants, birds and animals.

Activity 1: Daily lives of animals
For the children to start thinking about what changes take place over each 24-hour period in the lives of living creatures, they can start with themselves.

They can record in pictures their main activities over one 24-hour period on copymaster 15. They can then record the 24-hour pattern for another creature on a second copy of the copymaster (e.g. a pet dog, or a 'wild' creature they have researched in the books, such as a mouse or robin).

Results and discussion should reveal the effects of night and day (though humans cheat somewhat by lighting and heating their homes). The children could be helped to speculate on times past when we were more at the mercy of 'natural' light and temperatures.

Activity 2: A case study
This is quite a complex piece of research to do, and as it has to be done over a period of time, will depend on your encouragement and organisation to keep going. The task is to choose a tree or animal and look at the effect of seasonal changes on the thing you have chosen. If it is done by direct observation, which is probably the best way, then the children need to systematically record information in each of the four seasons of the year.

For example, they may choose a holly or oak tree in the school grounds. If there is no available living thing which they can observe directly, they can research an animal (e.g. swallow or hedgehog) and write about that. It may be best to let them do this work from secondary sources in four stages, so that they can 'feel' the seasons in turn as they write about them.

It is probably best if they complete a new copymaster 16 for each season.

A day in the life of Elaine Brooks (Lisa's mum)

7am	9am	10am	12 noon	2pm	4pm	6pm	8pm	10pm
Make tea Call children	School run Shop Cook lunch Take Norman to Tots	Go to work	Fetch Norman from Tots Feed Norman	Go to park Call on Mrs Bloggs	Fetch children Help with homework	Cook tea	Watch TV Ironing Letters	Bed

A day in the life of The Female Hirundo Rustica (Swallow)

5am	6am		8pm
Clean nest	Feed babies	————————→	Sleep

HUMANS AND THE EARTH'S SURFACE C17

Area of study 5 P of S 3b

Purpose
To demonstrate that humans change the local land-scape.

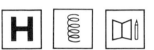

Materials needed
Information related to local development projects or building projects, drawing paper and pencils, camera and film; books on arable farming.

Activity 1: Observing man-made change
This activity will depend on the location of your school and plans in the area. It could be that you can see the reclamation of coastline, the building of a section of motorway or a housing estate. Any of these projects can be watched over time. If there are no such projects nearby or if trips out are not possible, then you will have to collect (in advance) a dossier of pictures about a project, and 'before' and 'after' pictures of the landscape. It is possible that maps and street plans may show these changes. The children can construct 'before' and 'after' models of that piece of landscape.

If you wish, the children can draw a view of the landscape before and after the man-made changes on copymaster 17.

Our local landscape before the factory was built

Our local landscape after the factory was built

Activity 2: A new building seen as environmental change
If possible let the children observe the erection of a new building, by taking them along to look and draw the changes every few days. You will need to arrange this with the owner of the property, and the senior

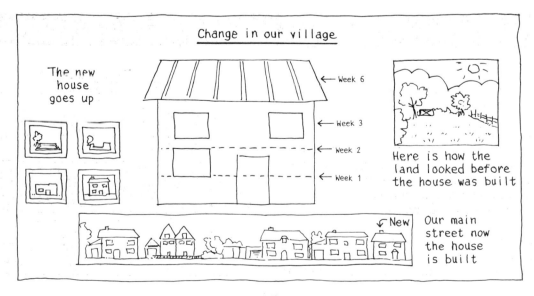

Change in our village

The new house goes up

← Week 6
← Week 3
← Week 2
← Week 1

Here is how the land looked before the house was built

New
Our main street now the house is built

person on site. Also, do make sure that the children stand at a safe distance to watch. Their drawings can be displayed, and you can trace over one set and superimpose each stage on top of the other to show the 'growth' of the building over time. If you take some photographs too, the children can see the effects of the man-made change on the whole street.

Activity 3: Local use of land

Look with the children at the use made of the land locally. If you work in an inner-city school take the children to the nearest open country, or if this is not possible go and take photographs of the local landscape. Let the children look at maps of the area, and list and talk about what human beings are doing to the land. There may be positive effects of the work of man, including some of the following examples:

  Organic farming
● Preservation schemes, tree renewal and hedge maintenance
● Landscaping of tips and slag heaps
● Creation of new features like reservoirs (some

people may see this as a negative effect, particularly as natural habitats and features are destroyed).

There may also be negative effects of the work of man, including some of the following:

● Deforestation
● Unsightly quarries, industrial sites and rubbish tips
● Chemical intervention in attempts to improve crop yields
● Destruction of 'natural countryside' in the construction of golf courses and other leisure activity sites
● Motorway construction.

Activity 4: The farmer's year

Visit a local farm with the children during each of the four seasons of the year. The children can create a 'farmer's diary' for a typical year, listing changes in what a farmer does as the year passes. If the children cannot see a farmer at work, consult books about farming and let them draw what they think an arable farmer does to the land over the passage of a year.

Area of study 6	P of S 3d	**HUMANS AND THE AIR**

Purpose

To show that humans pollute the Earth's atmosphere.

Materials needed

Pictures of factory chimneys emitting smoke and fumes; publicity material about petrol fumes and

unleaded petrol; anti-smoking leaflets.

Activity 1: Clean air

Look at the available information with the children and discuss its implications. The children can devise their own 'clean air' posters for display.

Pollution changes our world and us

Area of study 7	P of S 3d	**HUMANS, RIVERS AND COASTAL WATERS**

Purpose

To show that waste humans create is being discharged into rivers and seas, causing pollution.

Materials needed

A nearby river or stream, river monitoring station, or a strip of coastline with an accessible high-tide mark; rubbish bags and a large jar for a water sample, rubber gloves; a visitor from a 'clean up rivers' organisation; books about the state of our rivers.

Activity 1: River or sea inspection

If you are lucky enough to live near a suitable river or on the coast, the children can take a stretch of river or

River search

We looked at the River Dan in our town

shoreline, perhaps about 10 m long, and firstly look at its general features, then at what lives and grows there. Then they can collect any rubbish there is and collect a sample of water. Back in the classroom they can collate their findings, examine, draw and weigh the rubbish and inspect the water. Remember there may be health risks here, so supply rubber gloves if necessary. Their resulting work can be displayed, and if their results are alarming, they could be sent to the owners of the water or land for their attention.

Activity 2: River monitoring
Invite someone from the river authority to come and talk to the children about measures which are being taken to clean up the rivers.

IMPROVING THE ENVIRONMENT

Area of study 8 — P of S 3d — C18

Purpose
To devise and adopt a scheme for improving the environment.

Materials needed
Garden tools, seeds and plants, rubbish bags; a range of waste packaging including cardboard, plastic, cans, newspapers and bottles.

Activity 1: The school garden
With the head and governors' permission take over a plot in the school garden and transform it into, for example, a scented garden, a garden attracting butterflies, a wild flower garden. There may be capitation money or PTA money to finance this, or a local garden centre may sponsor you. If there is no land available belonging to the school, you can use plant troughs and large pots to produce miniature gardens. If you start a project like this, be prepared to put in much extra time yourself. The children will be keen and willing, but will find it difficult to be enthusiastic about routine weeding. The progress of the project can be monitored by the children themselves, and their resulting work can be displayed to advantage. It can also become a continuing school resource and a school garden log-book can be started, which will be added to by succeeding generations of children.

Activity 2: Litter campaign
With your help the children can mark out a cluster of roads near the school. With adult help, they can scour the pavements, kerbs and hedges for litter. The resulting haul (collected in black rubbish bags) can be placed where all can see. The children can combine this result with a request to local householders about litter. With adult help leaflets can be distributed. Every child in the school can be given one to take home. This would be a suitable 'project' for a school video.

Activity 3: Discussion and sorting of waste
Remind the children that some packaging can be recycled. Talk about bottle banks and newspaper collection points. Ask them if they can offer to assemble these things regularly in their own home, ready for a trip to local collection points.

The children can make a collection of re-usable waste for a specified fortnight at home, and when they have collected it all, record how much of each kind of waste is produced.

The recording can be done on copymaster 18.

Activity 4: Official recycling
Ask the local department of environmental health if it is possible for someone to come and speak to the children about what happens to household waste, what can be recycled and how.

Activity 5: Supermarket packaging
With the co-operation of a local supermarket, ask if you and the children may look at and list the packaging materials found in a typical supermarket trolley of shopping. The supermarket manager may be helpful if your visit can receive publicity in the local paper. The children can work out how much packaging is recyclable.

FERTILISERS AND THE ENVIRONMENT

Area of study 9 | P of S 3d | C19

Purpose
To formulate opinions about fertilisers and the environment, and to get the children to back up their arguments with information based on their own experience.

Materials needed
A list of the constituents of some fertilisers, letter-writing materials.

Activity 1: Fertilisers and agriculture
Either visit a farm where chemical fertilisers are used, or invite a farmer to visit you. Observe and discuss the changes made by chemical fertilisers.

Activity 2: Production of fertilisers
Write to a major producer of fertilisers and ask them for publicity material about their range of natural and man-made products. Examine and discuss the implications of the advertising material.

Activity 3: Organic farming and gardening
Visit an organic garden. Find out what is done to get a good yield and what problems there are.
    Copymaster 19 can be used for consolidation.

PLANTS' NEEDS: LIGHT, WATER, WARMTH

Area of study 10 | P of S 1b | C20, 21

Purpose
To establish plants' needs for light, water and warmth to grow.

Materials needed
Seeds, flowerpots, potting compost, large pot or thick paper to enclose a flowerpot completely, calibrated jug for watering; propagator.

Activity 1: Light is necessary
Set up an experiment like that in *Life-sustaining conditions* at Level 2 (Area of Study 1, page 10). This time plant up two pots with grass, cress or beans in similar quantities of soil or potting compost. Subject them to the same growing conditions (side by side on the same site) and water them with the same volume of water at regular intervals, from a calibrated jug.

Enclose one pot completely so that no light reaches the seedlings. Expose the other pot to natural light.
    Let the children monitor what happens by inspecting the pots at intervals and recording their observations. Make the intervals perhaps every two or three days. They need to record the day on which shoots emerged, the colour and general appearance of the seedlings (whether they look healthy and robust or 'weedy' and thin). They can also write down the amount of water given and the amount and rate of growth, if any.
    Results should show the following:

● Little or no growth in the pot which is left in darkness or forced whitish shoots which eventually fail to thrive
● Vigorous growth in the pot exposed to light.

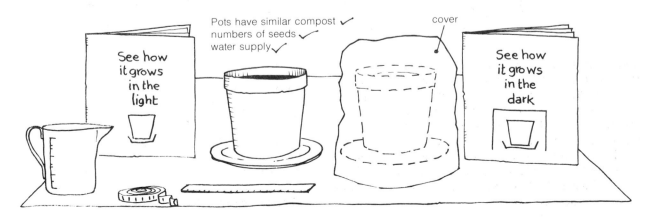

Activity 2: Varying the amount of light

Try planting up three pots with seeds and put one on the windowsill in full light, one in a shady place and one in the stock cupboard, or conditions of almost total darkness. Ask the children to water the pots at regular intervals with similar volumes of water, but otherwise leave them undisturbed.

Results should show that in all pots the seedlings lean towards any light source available. The pot in the shade can be turned around once the seedlings have started to lean towards the light, and they should, given time, lean the other way.

Copymaster 20 is a record sheet for this experiment.

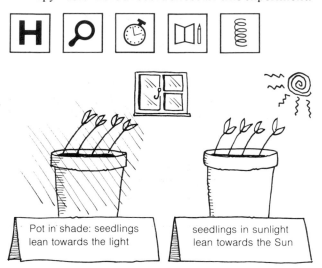

Pot in shade: seedlings lean towards the light

seedlings in sunlight lean towards the Sun

Activity 3: Varying the amount of water

Plant up three pots with similar quantities of compost or earth and put some seeds in them. Leave the pots side by side in the light. Let the children water two of the pots at intervals, giving one pot enough water to leave the compost thoroughly moist and the other so much water that the seedlings are permanently water-logged. Leave the third pot entirely without water. Let the children record what happens, and draw conclusions. If the seeds you plant are water-tolerant they will thrive no matter how much water the children give them. Absence of water should inhibit growth markedly.

Copymaster 21 allows the children to record the experiment formally.

Activity 4: Varying the temperature

If possible, find two locations in school which contrast in temperature at all times, but where the light levels and amount of moisture in the air are likely to be similar. (Sensors would be very useful in establishing the optimum places in school which meet these criteria). Plant up two pots with similar compost and seeds and place one in each location. Give them similar quantities of water. After some growing time, it should be possible to see that heat helps growth (providing the seedlings are not exposed to too high a temperature).

Have a look at a commercial propagator, or make one using a vivarium or plastic box which can be covered with plastic sheeting. Discuss why these are used to 'bring on' germination or promote early growth. (If the children monitor the temperature inside and outside the propagator they should detect the temperature difference). Seeds can be grown in the propagator to prove the point, but remember to tell the children that the water vapour inside a closed propagator is confined, creating an atmosphere which is not only warm but also damp.

Attainment target 2: Life and living processes

Level 4	**Statements of attainment**	**Statements of attainment**

Pupils should:

a) be able to name and locate the major organs of the human body and of the flowering plant.

b) be able to assign plants and animals to their major groups using keys and observable features.

c) understand that the survival of plants and animals in an environment depends on successful competition for scarce resources.

d) understand food chains as a way of representing feeding relationships in an ecosystem.

Pupils could:

name and point to the approximate positions of organs such as heart, lungs, stomach, and kidneys in humans and the stamens and ovary of a flowering plant.

use a key to allocate animals to vertebrate groups and plants to groups such as ferns, conifers and flowering plants.

explain the need for woodland floor plants to grow and flower before trees bear leaves and block out the light.

for a particular habitat, order organisms in a food chain, such as oak tree – caterpillar – blue tit – sparrowhawk

---

Area of study 1 | **P of S 1a** | ## MAJOR ORGANS IN HUMANS AND PLANTS C22, 23

Purpose
To identify and name the organs in ourselves and in flowering plants.

Materials needed
Books, diagrams and models depicting the major organs in the human body; specimen flowering plants with flowers that can be sliced through for examination, craft knife, magnifiers, charts and books about flowering plants.

Activity 1: Organs in us
Show the children pictures, diagrams and models to identify the location of the major organs in the body: for example the heart, lungs, stomach, intestine, kidneys, reproductive organs and brain. Quiz the children to ensure they can point to themselves to show the location of these organs with reasonable accuracy.

Let the children complete some simple diagrams to show the location of these major organs.

Copymaster 22 is a body outline with some pictures of organs alongside. The children can draw arrows to the locations, or cut the drawings of organs out and stick them where they should go on the outline.

Activity 2: Organs in flowering plants
Let the children examine the flowering plants, including the flowers. These can be sliced in half and viewed through magnifiers. Plants having large single flower heads may prove easier for the children to work on. Examples include daffodils, tulips, daisies and dandelions. The children can draw what they see and research the names of the plant organs.

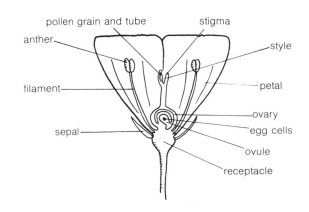

Copymaster 23 is a drawing of a flowering plant ready for labelling.

| Area of study 2 | P of S 1c | | **OUR BODY HEALTH** | C24, 25 |

Purpose

To show how the body can be kept healthy by its own defence systems, by eating sufficient food in a balanced diet, by regular teeth cleaning and the avoidance of tobacco, alcohol and other drugs.

Materials needed

Books and charts about the body's defence systems, and about germs; information from charity organisations about the malnutrition suffered in some parts of the world; diet and health information (possibly available through the school doctor); data about dental health (possibly from the school dentist); reference books about health and fitness, a timer or watch with a minute hand; information packs about smoking, drinking and other drugs.

Activity 1: The body's defence system

Discuss what happens when we feel ill or cut ourselves. Let the children chart the body's processes in recovery, including things such as leucocytes and the formation of scabs. Mention also the help we give our bodies by using, for example, antiseptics and first-aid dressings.

Copymaster 24 can be used to record the restoration process which follows a minor accident such as a cut on the finger.

Activity 2: Microbes and disease

Explain the association between bacteria and viruses and the symptoms they cause in us. Discuss preventive measures such as eating a balanced diet and keeping warm.

Activity 3: Finding out about malnutrition

Look at available literature on inadequate diet and malnutrition. Discuss the fact that although in Britain the majority of us may all eat enough, we also need to eat a balance of the right things.

Activity 4: Components of a healthy diet

Revise what the children did at Level 2, reminding them of the four main food groups and what to include in their daily intake. Discuss the avoidance of too much sugar, fats and additives. They can devise a day's menu, to include foods they like and which are good for them.

Copymaster 25 provides a menu headings list.

Activity 5: Action for healthy teeth

Ask the school dentist or nurse if they will pay a visit to the class to discuss dental health. With the children decide on a number of points to put in a plan for action. Display the outcomes along with dental care information (see below).

Activity 6: Exercise and fitness

Talk to the children about what they think exercise is, and what it does. Let them measure their own pulse rate before exercise, by holding the inside of their wrist with two fingers while applying pressure on the back of the wrist with the thumb. They will need a timer or

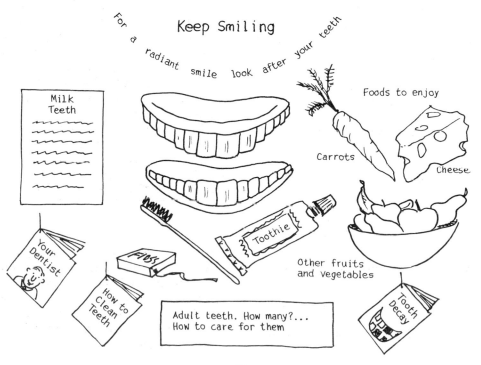

Keep Smiling

For a radiant smile look after your teeth

Milk Teeth

Foods to enjoy

Carrots

Cheese

Toothie

Other fruits and vegetables

Your Dentist

How to Clean Teeth

Adult teeth. How many?... How to care for them

Tooth Decay

watch with a second hand. If they time their pulse for 30 seconds they can work out the rate per minute. Then ask them to run on the spot for a couple of minutes before retaking their pulse rate. The ensuing discussion may help them to understand the role of exercise in keeping the circulatory and respiratory systems working well, and that exercise can therefore help to prevent the onset of circulatory disorders.

Activity 7: Effects of tobacco and alcohol and other drugs
This is an area needing careful handling. Find out the statistics about health and drug-taking and give the children the plain facts. They will all know people, probably in their own family, who smoke and drink, so if you reveal strong opinions you may upset some families. Children do need to know however, at this age, the risks from activities such as smoking, drinking and sniffing glue.

Activity 8: Healthy life plans
Using appropriate literature about drugs (including nicotine and alcohol) ask the children firstly to write a list of dos and don'ts for a healthy life, and secondly to write some advertising material for any 'anti' campaign of their choice.

GROUPING LIVING THINGS

C26

Purpose
To show that creatures can be put into groups, and show how they may be grouped, using keys.

Materials needed
A selection of plants, for example flowering grasses or plants 'borrowed' from a garden centre, or a selection of mini-beasts; a computer, data base software and reference books about the whole animal and plant world.

Activity 1: Similarities and differences
The children need to observe closely and compare a range of plants or mini-beasts to find out similarities and differences. Then they can start to assemble the trails in a sort of treasure hunt. For example, a simple key, for a collection of snails, slugs, earthworms, beetles, woodlice and millipedes may run like the flowchart below.

The key can then be developed further to identify different kinds of beetle, for example. Each time the children think they have the next distinguishing feature in the trail, they can put it to the test with one of their specimens and see if it works. You should relate this work to that on decision-making trees in Mathematics AT5 Level 4.

Once the children have developed their own 'keys' they should be shown some of the standard ones available. They should also have the chance to look at books about animals to discover the ways in which these are commonly grouped.

Activity 2: Creating a data base about mammals
This activity involves accessing information on the computer and so is best done with children in groups of only two or three. Firstly the children need to research their information. In order to make the information manageable let them choose five mammals for study. In rough they should write down a description of the important features and habits of each animal. Then they can find labels for things they have looked at in all the creatures, e.g. covering: fur or hair. Their data base will start with labels such as these:

- Data base: Mammals
- Name of animal
- Size in cm
- Covering
- Live babies/eggs
- How many young at a time
- Blood (warm/cold)

When their data base is complete, they can print out all their information and store their data on disk. The next group of children can do the same task. When several groups of children have had a go they can compare their data bases and see if they can be amalgamated (with your help). Then the computer will have sufficient entries for the children to access their data base and print out sub-groups of animals, e.g. those mammals which commonly have more than three babies at a time.

Copymaster 26 will remind them of some of the details on their data base.

Activity 3: Choosing and creating a data base
Ask the children to construct a sophisticated data base on the computer. They can devise it themselves, for at least 20 living creatures. They can then access that data base and do sorts according to characteristics.

They can compare their own key with available published keys.

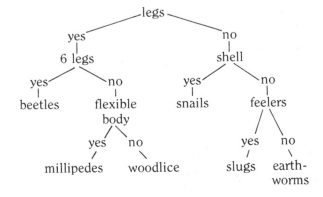

Activity 4: Creature quiz

Ask the children to compile a quiz on animal characteristics, using the information they collected for their own data base. They can then test their classmates.

Purpose

To establish that animals of the same species vary one from another.

Materials needed

Some pets, either school pets or ones belonging to the children (several of each species); tape measures, large scales or weighing machine, magnifiers, pencils and paper.

Activity 1: Animal comparisons

Look carefully at the two or more examples of a species, e.g. perhaps you could borrow three pet rabbits, in separate cages. Ask the children to list as many features of the appearance as they can, e.g. fur colour, length of whiskers, appearance of fur. Then under each heading they can describe and compare the rabbits they are looking at in relation to these features. They can then talk to the rabbits' owners and ask about features they cannot see such as preferred diet and sleeping habits.

Using copymaster 27 the children can rule a column for each pet examined and compare across the columns the characteristics for each pet (e.g. fur colour, length of ears).

Activity 2: Measuring animal comparisons

When they have completed Activity 1, the children can try to detect and measure more detailed differences, e.g. stray hairs can be measured and their length compared; if the parentage of the animals is known, that can also be compared. They can, with the owners' help, weigh each animal and also weigh the amount of food it will eat in a day. They can record and compare all these results in tabular form and comment on how much difference there is between the sample animals of the same species.

Copymaster 28 can be used to tabulate this information.

Activity 3: Comparing many animals of the same species

Collect together as much information as you can about the varieties within a species. A straightforward example might be to look at domestic dogs or cats. There may be a pet to look at and the children may already know something about them.

Purpose

To identify that plant families contain varieties which vary just as animal families do.

Materials needed

Books about plant classification and plant families; packets of seeds including two or three varieties of the same flowering plant.

Activity 1: Comparing growth in plants of the same family

Plant seeds of two or three varieties of the same flowering plant. Get the children to monitor germination time, speed of growth of the shoot, how the first leaves emerge. They can record this information, and transfer it to a class chart (see opposite).

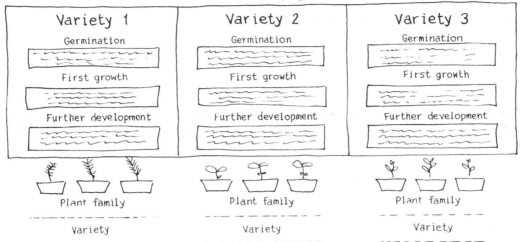

See how they grow

Variety 1	Variety 2	Variety 3
Germination	Germination	Germination
First growth	First growth	First growth
Further development	Further development	Further development
Plant family	Plant family	Plant family
Variety	Variety	Variety

Activity 2: Comparing flowers in plants of the same family

Using the plants grown for Activity 1, or using plants that have been grown in the school greenhouse or bought in from a garden centre, get the children to observe closely, draw, cut in section and describe the flowers. They can record their results in tabular form.

VARIATIONS IN VEGETABLE VARIETIES

Area of study 6 | P of S 2a

Purpose

To show that there is a wide range of variation within vegetable species.

Materials needed

Three kinds of outdoor tomato plants, named and labelled, and three kinds of french bean seed/plant or a similar vegetable; a caretaker gardener, or perhaps a parent who is a gardening enthusiast and who will keep an eye on the plants when the children are not there; growing bags or fertile garden plot, trowels and a watering can.

Activity 1: Comparing vegetables

Though the children can compare growth in the different plants, and will need to care for and stake them, the most important comparisons are to be made with the ripe vegetables. They can be observed, felt, weighed and (in the case of tomatoes) tasted. They can also be cut open to see if there are differences in colouring, shape and number of seeds inside. Again, results can be tabulated. When they begin to ripen one of the plants can be lifted and planted in a large pot to add to a class display.

FLORA AND FAUNA

Area of study 7 | P of S 3a

C29

Purpose

To show that physical differences and daily and seasonal changes are reflected in the kinds of plants and animals found in a location.

Materials needed

Fieldwork equipment such as clipboards and magnifiers, binoculars, collecting jars and bags; string and pegs for marking out observation areas.

Activity 1: The school perimeter fence

If your school has a lot of ground the children may not have explored along the perimeter fence or hedge. Even if they have done so at Level 2, they can now begin to make their observations systematic. Using the perimeter fence or hedge as a location for study, ask each pair of children to take a marked out metre, or more if you wish. Get them to look for all they can find in that small area. They can collect specimens, but be sure to remind them of the care with which to work, and return the creatures to the hedge after they have been available for the children to see for a short while. Help the children to produce a 'picture map' of the hedge, with each pair of children contributing their section. On it they can attach some of the following:

● Drawings of creatures, with their measurements and other comments
● Names and descriptions of plants, bushes and trees
● Signs of birds and larger animals
● Any daily changes likely at the location (for example, for that part of the hedge next to the school gate, the constant use of the gateway at 8.50 a.m. and 3.30 p.m. might affect both plants and animals in different ways.

Animals and plants in two localities

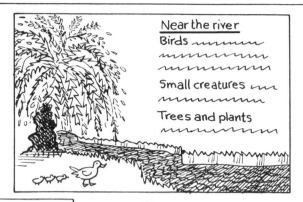

LOOK AND COMPARE

Activity 2: Localities in the landscape

Depending on the location of the school, arrange trips to two locations where the children can look at plants and signs of animals in open country. This may, for example, be in a river valley, on a mountain, in woods, in dunes or near a beach. Let the children apply all the observation skills they have already worked on, and record their observations. This should offer the chance for them to make comparisons between things seen in these differing localities. For example:

● Do the trees have different shapes? Are they different kinds of tree?
● Where are we likely to find worms, leatherjackets or spiders?
● What sorts of birds can be seen in the open country location compared with those around school?

The children need to note down as many things as they can about each location. They may include some of the following:

● Type of soil
● Type of underlying rock
● Landscape features (for example river basin, coastal dunes)

● Plants and trees
● Mini-beasts found
● Birds seen
● Signs of other animals
● Comments on daily changes occurring in each location
● Comments on what the seasonal changes are/are expected to be at the location.

The children can then set side by side their reports on the two locations and make comparisons.

Copymaster 29 allows the children to compare localities.

Activity 3: Comparing two countries

Using the reference books, choose two countries with widely differing terrain and climate. Ask the children to write a comparative study of the flora and fauna, relating the presence of these species to the physical conditions.

 | Area of study 8 | P of S 3a |

ENVIRONMENTAL CHANGE

 C30

Purpose

To show how to measure changes in the environment using a variety of instruments, and to discuss some of their effects on us.

Materials needed

Tape recorders and cassettes, light meter, camera with built in light meter and film, access to school boiler room or central heating control room; advertising material about electronic heating control, Celsius thermometers.

Activity 1: Sound levels

Together with the children, plan and record the sounds of a school day. The children may wish to try controlling a selection of variables, and they could work in groups to devise a recording sequence where, for example, the location is fixed, they record only voices, or they record only noises outside school which may impinge, such as aircraft, traffic or roadworks. They may choose to be selective, to match their sound track to a journalistic account of the school day, or they may fix a time interval between recordings and look at changes in noise levels. In groups they should be able to plan and execute an experiment and then give a presentation of results.

Activity 2: Light levels

Let the children use a light meter at a fixed location in the classroom to detect changes in light levels throughout a school day. If the children use a light meter that is built into a camera, and take a photo at each light check, you will need to discuss with them the connection between the size of aperture and available light.

Activity 3: Temperature control

Find out how the school heating system works. Ask the caretaker to show the children the boilers and the controls, including thermostats. Look through advertising material about electronic heating system thermostats, available from electricity and gas showrooms and appliance shops.

Activity 4: Temperature change

Let the children use a Celsius thermometer in a fixed location, to check the classroom temperature throughout a school day. The use of thermometers is also part of the work the children do in AT3, Level 4, and AT4, Level 2, so there are possibilities for combined work at this Level. They can record temperature changes and comment in writing on how they can account for the changes over the day, which may include things such as school heating, position of the Sun, open windows and doors, presence or absence of people and so on.

Copymaster 30 can be used to record these observations.

Activity 5: Effects of change on us

Review the work the children have done in previous Activities and discuss some of the possible effects on us of environmental changes. For example, if it is too noisy near the hall to work, the class may move to another part of the school. Compare our management of our environment (by, for example, heating, lighting and soundproofing) with the lack of control that other animals have. Ask the children to reflect on the likely effects of environmental changes on animals.

 P of S 3c # SURVIVAL AND SCARCE RESOURCES

Purpose

To show that creatures only survive in habitats where their needs are adequately met, and that if resources become too scarce species have to move to another location, or become extinct.

Materials needed

A visiting garden expert, pictures and books about animals in their natural habitats; books about recently extinct species and information about wildlife in danger of extinction.

Activity 1: Plants

Ask a local gardening expert, or a colleague or parent who is a keen gardener to come and talk to the children about where cultivated plants are sited in order that they grow well. For example, smaller sun-loving plants are put at the front of borders rather than under the spreading branches of taller plants at the back which may exclude too much light. Plants with shallow root systems needing a lot of water may preclude the planting of others too close to them.

Activity 2: Animals

Choose some animals, locally occurring ones if possible, and talk about their need in terms of the habitat required and why they live where they do.

Examples might include squirrels who live in parks where there are oak and hazel trees, birds of prey who often haunt fields of cereal crops, motorway verges where mice and other small mammals live and sea gulls, some of whom have sought a life inland where rubbish tips are a ready food supply for such scavengers.

Activity 3: Losers in the struggle to survive

If vital resources become scarce, animals move away or risk extinction. Find out about some of the creatures that have become extinct during the last two centuries,

Recently Extinct

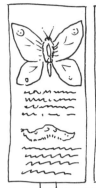

The Dodo

Extinct because:

The climate changed? Perhaps

Hunted or shot? Perhaps

The food became scarce? Perhaps

ask the children to draw them and try to discover from the books why the creatures became extinct. Climatic changes, the loss of foodstuffs, man's encroachment on habitats and hunting may all be possible reasons for extinction. Complete a 'recently extinct' dossier or create a home-made wallchart display.

Activity 4: Likely losers

Let the children choose a threatened species and find out all they can about its needs. It may be, for example, a bird, butterfly, whale or white rhino. The activity may be started with a display.

Ask them to devise a ten-point action plan to help prevent extinction. Invite someone from a local naturalists' trust or a local radio natural history team to come and give the children advice and help.

Copymaster 31 can be used to record their action plan.

Going, going, gone
These living things may soon be extinct

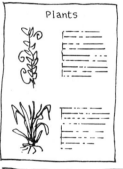

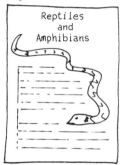
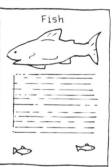

Plants Insects and others Reptiles and Amphibians Fish

Other living creatures at risk

Panda   Gorilla   Rhino   Big cats   Elephant   Whale   Wolf

FOSSILS

Purpose
To show what fossils are and how they came about.

Materials needed
Books and charts about early life forms, museum exhibits including fossils and footprint casts, Plasticine® or clay; leaves, Vaseline®, hard plastic sheet, plaster of Paris; puppet making materials.

Activity 1: Fossils
Assemble a collection of fossils from a museum and/or borrowed from parents and children. Create a display.

Let the children examine and handle the fossils over a period of days. Then let them experiment with rubbings and chalks to produce accurate drawings.

Let the children use copymaster 32 to draw an outline of some fossils and do drawings of what they think the creatures looked like when alive.

Then label the fossils and the children can look up

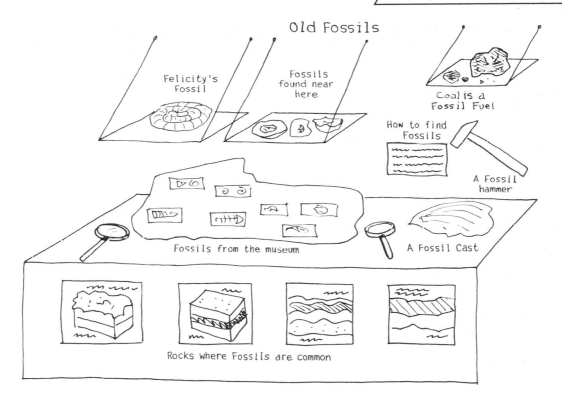

what they actually looked like. Discuss the kinds of creatures that might be preserved as fossils.

Activity 2: Coal
Look at a lump of coal and examine a time chart to find out how long ago the tree was alive. Some coal may contain leaf fossils.

Activity 3: Making plaster casts
Try making casts of foot and handprints and the prints of leaves to display alongside fossil print exhibits. There are casts of dinosaur prints to be seen in museums throughout the country. These would be a good source of comparison with those of members of the class! Make casts by placing a large lump of clay or Plasticine® in a shallow tray. Press the hand (or whatever is making the cast) into the clay. Fill the cast with plaster of Paris which has just been mixed. BE QUICK! It sets rapidly. Leave until hard, and peel off the clay.

Activity 4: Making an imprint
Apply grease all over some leaves and place them on a plastic sheet. Build a 'boundary wall' of Plasticine® or clay a few centimetres high around the leaves. Pour in mixed plaster of Paris and leave until completely dry. Peel away the clay, turn over the plaster and lift off the leaves. There should be imprints of the leaves for the children to see. Some fossils were made by a layer of silt covering leaves or animals. The silt eventually hardened into sedimentary rock.

Activity 5: How fossils formed
Discuss with the children the ways in which fossils have been formed. These include those the children may already have talked about in Activities 1–4 above: the formation of a cast and carbonisation. Other methods include mineralisation of the bones and refrigeration (hence fossil mammoths).

Activity 6: Identifying the dinosaurs
If possible, before the children consult the secondary sources, let them do some detective work. Show them a cast of a dinosaur footprint or part of a bone and ask them to speculate on what the creature may have looked like. Get them to draw it and then show them what the experts think it looked like. Tell them what clues the experts used and what size the creature was, by comparing it with the school, a bus or something else of a suitable size. The children can then be placed in groups. Each group can choose a different dinosaur, research it and write up about when it lived, its appearance, diet and how it moved. They can also try and trace where remains have been found and in which museums fossils are on show. The results of the enquiry can be entered in a group book which can be displayed and then consulted by all the children. It can be added to school resources.

Activity 7: The dinosaurs' demise
Ask the children to research possible reasons why there are no dinosaurs around today. They can be helped to make glove or stick puppets representing the Sun, swamp, named plants and, for example, a Stegosaurus, Pterodactyl and Tyrannosaurus Rex. They can then enact the possible set of circumstances which led to extinction. This is probably better scripted than left to improvisation and, if it turns out well, could be put on video for use with other groups.

Activity 8: Long-extinct but not a dinosaur
Invite a member of a museum's staff to come and talk to the children about long-extinct life forms such as

35

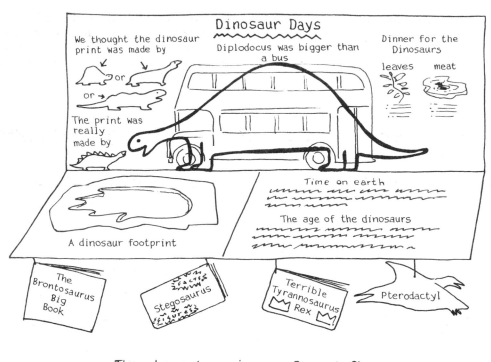

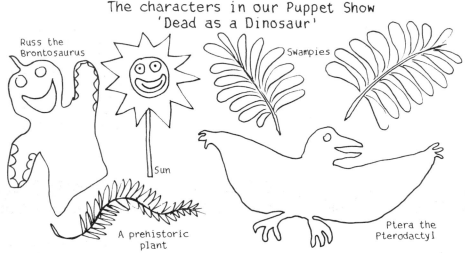

the precursors of the horse. Alternatively, research this with the help of the children and get them to develop expertise on 'Creatures in the past'.

Copymaster 33 can be used for each child to record

work about an extinct creature of their own choice, which may be, but need not necessarily be a dinosaur.

| Area of study 11 | P of S 4a | **FOOD CHAINS** |

Purpose
To explain the idea of a food chain.

Materials needed
Information packs about endangered species and reference books about food chains.

Activity 1: Food chains
Study food chains in the animal world, looking carefully at the diet, size, habitat and living habits of

the creatures. The children should be aware of the delicate balance in nature between the species found in food chains.

Plants are the primary producers in food chains and all animals are directly or indirectly dependent on plants. Discuss the implications of this for the care of plant resources on our planet.

The children can also look at a wide variety of plants and animals and establish whether they are part of a food chain or not. Not all animals are predators or prey.

Examples of food chains might include these:

Bird ⟶ caterpillar ⟶ cabbage
Snake ⟶ mouse ⟶ wheat
Finally the children can look at man's place in

relation to the natural world, and man as predator for sport or gain. They can discuss and develop views on the endangered species and what action, if any, humans should take to prevent their extinction.

Attainment target 2: Life and living processes

Level 5	Statements of attainment	Statements of attainment
	Pupils should:	Pupils could:
	a) be able to name and outline the functions of the major organs and organ systems in mammals and in flowering plants.	*explain how the heart acts as a pump in the body to circulate blood to the organs and that in a plant the roots provide anchorage and provide for the uptake of water and mineral salts.*
	b) know that information in the form of genes is passed on from one generation to the next.	*use information from an extended family (humans, guinea-pigs, rabbits) to show that a feature may be inherited.*
	c) know how pollution can affect the survival of organisms.	*explain how the level of pollution affects the survival of lichens by comparing the abundance and variety found in areas of high and low levels of air pollution.*
	d) know about the key factors in the process of decay.	*explain how to produce good quality compost from garden waste.*

  ORGAN SYSTEMS IN MAMMALS

Area of study 1 — P of S 1a — C34

Purpose
To name and know the function of the major organ system in mammals.

Materials needed
Books and charts about the major organ systems in ourselves and some other mammals.

Activity 1: Respiration
Find out what the children know about respiration. Make sure they understand that we need oxygen from the air to live, and that it is taken into our bodies via the blood stream from our lungs. Each time we take a breath we refill our lungs with air from which some of the oxygen is then taken up. When we do strenuous exercise like running, we breathe faster to pull more oxygen supplies into our bodies.

Let the children copy a drawing or diagram of our respiratory system.

Discuss the process by which de-oxygenated blood is pumped to the lungs by the heart, and returned to the heart when oxygenated to be pumped around the body.

Compare the respiratory systems of other mammals with our own by looking at books about mammalian anatomy and physiology.

Activity 2: Circulation
Show the children pictures and diagrams of our circulatory system. In discussion raise at least the following points:

● The blood system is a travel system in the body; it collects and takes food and oxygen to the organs
● The heart is a pump which drives the system
● The heart pumps blood to and from the lungs to get oxygen, and to and from all the parts of the body to supply oxygen and other nutrients
● Blood vessels are called arteries and veins; name some of the principal ones
● Some veins are nearer the body surface than arteries and the body temperature is regulated by some heat loss from these
● Oxygen makes arterial blood lighter in colour than venous blood
● Venous blood can flow less copiously than arterial blood because it has travelled far from the 'push' it received from the heart pump.

Let the children reproduce a diagram of the heart and major blood vessels. Compare their diagrams with pictures of the same system in other mammals.

Activity 3: Digestion

Show the children a model or chart of the human digestive tract. Tell them what the component parts are called and what they do. Ensure that the children understand that food is made soluble in the digestive process in order to enter the blood stream and so reach all parts of the body. Give the children a diagram to complete, showing the progress through the digestive tract.

Discuss the similarities and differences between ourselves and other mammals, for example dogs and cats; and those dissimilar like ruminants which have a four-part stomach to enable them to digest grass (for example cows, deer, giraffes and sheep).

Activity 4: Reproduction

Let parents know before you undertake this Activity. Tell the children the names of the reproductive organs in the human male and female and the main steps in reproduction. Include fertilisation, the growth of the foetus and some information about pregnancy and birth.

Ask the children to choose a mammal, other than themselves, and make a study of its reproductive system and cycle, including the gestation period and number of babies. Take the children to visit a farm or country park where there are baby animals.

Copymaster 34 has diagrams of the systems discussed in Activities 1–4; these can be used for the basis of discussion or labelling.

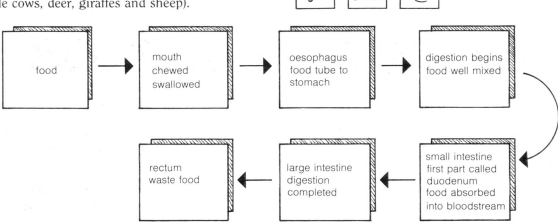

The digestive process

Area of study	P of S	
2	1a	**ORGAN SYSTEMS IN PLANTS** ▶

Purpose
To identify and know the functions of the major organ systems in flowering plants.

Materials needed
Books and pictures about plants and specimens of flowering plants, including sections of them, magnifiers; celery or a carnation and a vessel of water, food colouring; seeds of flowering plants, for example sunflowers or marrows, some snowdrop or daffodil bulbs, a growing medium and pots.

Activity 1: Organ systems
Show the children how to do drawings of flowering plants, from direct observation and using magnifiers. Use some of their detailed drawings and the specimens available to help them identify the major organ systems. Consult library resources and botany charts to ensure appropriate labelling.

Activity 2: Organ functions: Photosynthesis
Using carbon dioxide, sunshine and water green plants produce food molecules. Chlorophyll enables

the energy in sunlight to be used to split water molecules. Oxygen is given off. This is called the light reaction.

The hydrogen from the water is then used to convert carbon dioxide into carbohydrates (food). This reaction is called 'dark' for it does not require sunlight. Let the children find out how this happens and which parts of the plant are necessarily involved.

Activity 3: Organ functions: Circulation
To demonstrate that water is taken up by a plant, put a stick of celery or a white carnation into water with a little red food colouring in it, and leave it standing in the coloured water. After a while both celery and flower will have turned pink.

Activity 4: Organ functions: Reproduction
Get the children to plant the seeds and bulbs at the appropriate time of year, either in pots or in the school garden.

a) Seeds
● Follow seed packet instructions on planting and propagation.

- Observe the growth and development through the production of flowers and fruits.
- When the fruits should ripen, remove seeds and keep them in dry conditions for planting the following year.

b) Bulbs

- Measure the circumference of the bulbs before planting.
- Plant in bulb fibre or other suitable medium, or if they are planted in the ground, make sure the soil is light around each bulb.
- Observe the growth and development through the production of flowers.
- Leave the bulb plants until the foliage has died away and then examine for size increase, indicating vegetative reproduction.

If your class is a year group class or Y6, individual children may not be able to see through the whole Activity to the replanting of seeds. It is important that they are able to see the process through, and you may consider sending them a newsletter telling them of the growth patterns of seeds they grew, or taking specimens of a subsequent generation of plants along to their secondary school to show them.

Activity 5: Seed dispersal

This provides a well-documented and discrete topic that an individual child or children may like to carry through. Using all their research skills, school resources and field work, investigate the methods of seed dispersal, including, for example, wind, explosive pods, birds eating them, being carried in the fur of animals, or by streams.

Area of study 3	P of S 2c	FAMILY LIKENESS	C35

Purpose
To identify similarities between people in the same family, and between animal and plant families.

Materials needed
Photographs brought in by the children of themselves and members of their families.

Activity 1: Look-alikes in the family
Remind the children of their work at Level 2. The children can sift through the photographs for likenesses between members of their families. These can be placed on display for all to see, alongside an 'identikit' of clues to look for. They may be able to note, e.g. that most children of dark-haired parents have dark hair, and that sometimes children look more like their grandparents than their parents.

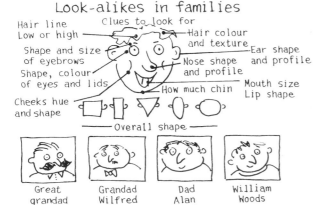

Look-alikes in families

4 generations of Woods
Spot the likeness!

Activity 2: Personality likenesses in the family
The children should discuss the idea at home and report back. For example, Cleo may say that her mum says she has her dad's temper, her auntie's friendly ways and her grandad's brains. Help them to look at a wide range of personality characteristics, but do not let them take this analysis too seriously.

Activity 3: Family habits and mannerisms
The children will need to discuss this at home. It does seem to be the case that even things we do not think can be passed on from one person to another, such as chewing the lip or tweaking the thumbs, do sometimes recur in families. Again, this should be fairly light-hearted, as it has not yet been established exactly what is transmitted from one generation to the next.

The children can do a survey among family members, if you first ask their parents' permission. They can devise the questions they would like to ask, and collate them afterwards.

They can use copymaster 35 to collect information.

Activity 4: Genes
Tell the children that family likenesses are the result of the passing on of characteristics from one generation to the next. The information is carried by genes in the sperm and egg. There is an opportunity here to do work on codes and ciphers.

Activity 5: Animal family likeness
Ask an animal expert like a vet, pet shop owner or RSPCA worker to come along and tell the children about the likenesses within litters of animals. Ask them to bring some slides, or borrow slides or pet care film which will demonstrate to the children family likeness in animals.

Activity 6: Plant family likeness

Research the famous work of Gregor Mendel, 1822–84, the founder of genetics. He did many experiments on pea plants, to show how characteristics were passed on to successive generations. One of the things he looked at was smooth appearance versus wrinkled. He found smooth was *dominant*, for peas that carried both smooth and wrinkled genes appeared smooth. The wrinkled gene was said to be *recessive*. Here is a chart which shows this trait in successive generations:

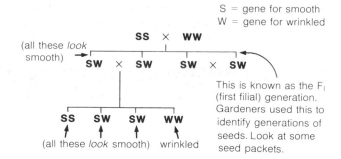

S = gene for smooth
W = gene for wrinkled

This is known as the F₁ (first filial) generation. Gardeners used this to identify generations of seeds. Look at some seed packets.

Area of study 4 | **P of S 3d**

ALL THE ISSUES IN POLLUTION

Purpose
To explain man's responsibility for pollution, its causes and outcomes.

Materials needed
Information about pollution from a wide range of sources including the Green party and protest groups; books and posters, tape recorders.

Activity 1: In-depth study of a kind of pollution
Ask the children to choose to study either the pollution of the air, the water or the land. They can then research this topic and produce a description of pollutants, their effects and an action list on preventing pollution. This work can be put into a folder for display. They can also write a personal statement about preventing this pollution and read this speech to the class, or record it on tape for their classmates to go and listen to.

Activity 2: The pollution debate
Ask the children to assemble information on one side or the other of a pollution issue, e.g. *against* smoking/ *for* individual choice; *against* discharge of industrial effluent into rivers/ *for* controlled discharge. Convene a formal debate to air both sides of the issue. The main arguments for and against each issue can be recorded on the two sides of a stand-up display which can be read from either side. Place it in the centre of the room so that the children can walk around it.

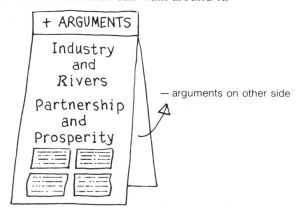

+ ARGUMENTS

Industry and Rivers

Partnership and Prosperity

— arguments on other side

Area of study 5 | **P of S 3d**

PLANNING AND POLLUTION

C36

Purpose
To identify and explain the issues both for and against a planning proposal.

Materials needed
Information about real planning proposals (local if possible). News about the outcomes of the submission of such proposals. Newspaper reports of projects having environmental impact, from initial plan to final implementation, tape recorders and a video camera, if available and appropriate.

Activity 1: Role-play: enquiry into an imaginary plan
Tell the children that they are to pretend a plan has been put before the local council to build, for example, a toy factory on the school playing field, or take out the hedges round the school and replace them with 10 m high metal fencing. The kind of plan you choose will depend on the location and appearance of your school. Some of the children can be local councillors, others residents, including children. Let the children assemble as many arguments as they can about their point of view and then role-play the enquiry. If appropriate, the proceedings can be recorded or put on video. Several children can also take minutes and write up a report on the enquiry.

If you wish, the people to be called to the enquiry can use copymaster 36 to record a character description, their vested interests, and arguments they are going to make.

Activity 2: The course of a genuine planning enquiry
This activity involves research and detective work, both on your part and the children's. Collection of information will take place over a long period of time. The children can then assemble a summary of the plan, a list of all the arguments put forward on either side and a summary of the outcomes. If the plan is current

and affects the immediate environment of the school, you may like to approach some local residents to see if they would be willing to come into school and be interviewed about their views on the plans. The interviews can be recorded and added to the school's resources.

DECAY

Purpose
To identify what happens when things decay.

Materials needed
Compost, flowerpots, sunflower or cress seeds; microscope slides of microbes.

Activity 1: An investigation of compost heaps
Consult the health and safety regulations before children dig in! Discuss the compost heaps they may have seen or have in their own garden. What do they think happens? Get them to ask someone who has a compost heap what he/she thinks happens. Try to obtain some mature, well-rotted compost and grow some sunflower seeds or cress in it alongside pots containing seeds in ordinary soil. The vigorous growth they see in the seeds growing in compost will help them to understand the circular process of decay and regeneration and the necessity, for example, of leaving rotten branches and dead leaves in the woods, so that the woods themselves survive. Tell the children about the work of the small creatures in the compost, and the sort of conditions they need to assist decomposition.

What happens in the compost heap

Activity 2: Microbes
Let the children see microbes, on slides you have bought or maybe borrowed from a secondary school. They can draw what they see under the microscope. Though it is easy to grow microbes in the classroom we do not recommend it as you should be certain that there is no health risk whatsoever before you do so, and that may be difficult to guarantee. You can tell them about the growth of microbes in the laboratory.

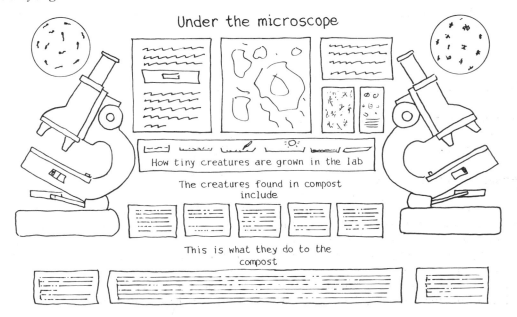

Under the microscope

How tiny creatures are grown in the lab

The creatures found in compost include

This is what they do to the compost

Pupils should develop knowledge and understanding of:

i the properties, classification and structure of materials;

ii explanations of the properties of materials;

iii chemical changes;

iv the Earth and its atmosphere.

Programme of study (relating to attainment target 3)

1a Pupils should investigate a number of different everyday materials, grouping them according to their characteristics. Properties such as strength, hardness, flexibility, compressibility, mass ('weight'), volume, and solubility should be investigated and related to everyday uses of the materials. Pupils should be given opportunities to compare a range of solids, liquids and gases and recognise the properties which enable classification of materials in this way.

Level 2	A/S 1	page 43
Level 3	A/S 1	page 46
Level 4	A/S 1	page 48

1b They should test the acidity and alkalinity of safe everyday solutions such as *lemon juice* using indicators which may be extracted from plants, such as *red cabbage*.

Level 5	A/S 2	page 57

1c They should know about the dangers associated with the use of some everyday materials including hot oil, bleach, cleaning agents and other household materials.

Level 2	A/S 1	page 43
Level 4	A/S 2	page 51

1d Experiments on dissolving and evaporation should lead to developing ideas about solutions and solubility.

Level 4	A/S 1	page 48

1e They should explore ways of separating and purifying mixtures such as muddy water, salty water and ink, by using evaporation, filtration and chromatography.

Level 5	A/S 1	page 56

3a Pupils should explore the origins of a range of materials in order to appreciate that some occur naturally while many are made from raw materials.

Level 3	A/S 2	page 47

3b They should investigate the action of heat on everyday materials resulting in permanent change: these might include cooking activities and firing clay.

Level 2	A/S 2	page 44

3c They should explore chemical changes in a number of everyday materials such as those that occur when mixing Plaster of Paris, mixing baking powder with vinegar and when iron rusts.

| Level 4 | A/S 3 | page 51 |
| Level 5 | A/S 3 | page 57 |

3d They should recognise that combustion of fuel releases energy and produces waste products including gases.

| Level 4 | A/S 4 | page 52 |
| Level 5 | A/S 3 | page 57 |

4a Pupils should have the opportunity to make regular, quantitative observations and keep records of weather and the seasons of the year. This should lead to a consideration of the water cycle.

Level 4	A/S 5	page 53
Level 4	A/S 6	page 54
Level 5	A/S 4	page 58

4b They should investigate natural materials (rocks, minerals, soils), sort them by simple criteria and relate them to their uses and origins. They should be aware of local distributions of some types of natural materials (sands, soils, rocks). They should observe, through fieldwork, how weather affects their surroundings, how sediment is produced and how soil develops.

Level 3	A/S 3	page 47
Level 4	A/S 7	page 55
Level 5	A/S 5	page 58

4c They should consider the major geological events which change the surface of the Earth and the evidence for these changes.

| Level 5 | A/S 5 | page 58 |

Attainment target 3: Materials and their properties

| Level 2 | | |

Statements of attainment

Pupils should:

a) be able to group materials according to observable features.

b) know that heating and cooling everyday materials can cause them to melt or solidify or change permanently.

Statements of attainment

Pupils could:

sort and group materials according to their shape, colour or hardness.

describe the formation and melting of ice and a cake mixture before and after baking.

| Area of study 1 | P of S 1a |

C37, 38

CHARACTERISTICS OF MATERIALS

Purpose
To identify some of the characteristics of materials.

Materials needed
A collection of naturally occurring and man-made materials, including, for example, rocks and pebbles, wood, straw, rubber, metal strips, clay, pottery, fabrics, glass, plastic. Include also salt, sugar, coal and liquids such as water, fruit juice and milk and a variety of mugs and jugs.

Activity 1: Comparison of materials
Assemble and lay out a collection of at least five kinds of material. Let the children handle the materials and compare them according to criteria they have decided on themselves. Discuss how they have decided to sort

them. Arrange the sorted items in a display. The following day ask the children to try sorting again, but differently. Repeat this process until the children have established many kinds of 'sort'.

The children can draw some examples of materials with various properties on copymaster 37.

Activity 2: The concept of transparency
Let the children look at a variety of glass and plastic samples. If necessary, tape the edges to prevent the children cutting themselves. You will need plain glass, patterned glass, frosted glass, coloured glass and opaque glass; see-through plastic, coloured plastic and opaque plastic. Packaging such as a jam jar, green and brown bottles and the plastic found in biscuit or chocolate boxes is of use, but you will also need to acquire some offcuts from a glazier. If they do not already know, explain the concept of transparency to them and get them to rank the samples in order of transparency. Ask them why we need some things to be transparent. Get them to name things in their home which are transparent.

Activity 3: Rank samples according to a characteristic
Choose a broad range of materials and ask the children to rank them in terms of hardness, flexibility (will they bend or stretch and spring back) and transparency in turn. The children can tabulate their results by drawing each item where it fits in the ranking.

Copymaster 38 can be used to record this work.

Activity 4: Safety and everyday materials
This discussion needs to be handled so that the children are not made over-anxious. Talk about taking care with everyday materials. Explain, for example, the dangers of boiling water and hot oil (which is very hot indeed – much hotter than boiling water). Point out that many items in the cleaning cupboard at home may be harmful to the skin, let alone our insides and should NEVER be smelled or tasted. Most cleaning powders and creams affect sensitive skin. Children should be encouraged to avoid them unless they have a grown up helping or watching.

 |

EFFECTS OF HEATING AND COOLING

Area of study 2 | P of S 3b | C39

Purpose
To show that materials sometimes change when warmed or cooled, and that the change can be permanent.

Materials needed
Fimo® or home-made play dough (made with two cups of flour to one of salt, with water and a little oil to mix, and some cream of tartar to stop it being sticky), ice-cubes and a freezer or freezer compartment of the fridge to re-freeze them, a candle in a holder and matches, a large bar of chocolate, plain biscuits, a saucepan and a wooden spoon, baking parchment, a table jelly, boiling water, a measuring jug and a bowl or individual containers (to set the jelly in).

Activity 1: What happens to model dough when we heat it?
Make some models from Fimo® or play dough. Fimo® is expensive but the colours are vivid and it holds its shape perfectly. Play dough is cheap but very soft and elastic, and it may prove difficult to make detailed impressions on it. The children could make models depicting some aspect of their work in other subjects. When the models are finished they need to be baked in an oven. Fimo® carries instructions. Play dough needs slow baking. The models can be painted and varnished. The children will observe that the dough which was soft and malleable retains neither of these characteristics after baking and in fact it becomes quite hard and brittle. This change is permanent. Display some raw dough and the finished models.

44

Dough | Models

We can change the shape of dough. It is stretchy and soft.

These models are hard and brittle. Take care!

To change soft dough to hard models we heat the dough in the oven.

Activity 2: The effects of heat and cold on water

Carefully heat some water in a pan or kettle without an automatic switch. As the water approaches boiling point discuss what happens when it boils. When it has been boiling for some time the children will be able to observe the steam and see that the level of the water in the pan has gone down (wait until it cools to show them this). Some of the water has 'gone'. Tell them that the steam is water vapour. As the water vapour cools it will turn back into water on cool surfaces such as the windows.

Now pour some water into an ice-tray and put it into the freezer or freezer compartment of the fridge to cool. When ice starts to form, get it out and show the children. Then return it to the freezer until cubes form. Take the ice-tray out. Put the ice-cubes into a bowl and observe what happens when they are left at room temperature. Discuss with the children the idea that liquid water becomes solid if it is made very cold, and turns back to liquid when warmed again.

Activity 3: The effect of heat on candle wax

Taking care that the children are at a safe distance, light a household candle. As the wax melts the children can see that it becomes liquid. You can let liquid drops drip onto a sheet of paper. When they are cool the children can see that as the hot wax cools it turns solid again.

Activity 4: The effect of heat on chocolate

Though the children will already be familiar with this, it is fun to do, and may therefore establish the solid–liquid–solid chain concept more readily than other experiments. Break the chocolate into a bowl and stand the bowl in a pan of hot water. Heat the pan if necessary to melt the chocolate. In order that everyone may have a taste, you may find it easiest to dip one end of some plain biscuits in the chocolate and lay them on baking parchment to cool. Alternatively, stir some cornflakes or rice krispies into the chocolate, and when bound together spoon out little mounds onto the baking parchment then leave them to set. Before they eat the evidence, make sure that the children have noted that solid chocolate melts to a liquid when heated and returns to solid when cooled.

Activity 5: The effect of heat on jelly

Show the children an unmade table jelly, or one that has been made up and set in a bowl. Make up the jelly according to the instructions, or tip the made up jelly into a pan and heat it until it melts. Then put the jelly into individual containers and leave to set. (One table jelly will make about eight small helpings). The children can take the jelly home for tea. They will also have noted that solid jelly, when warmed, becomes liquid and when cooled, becomes solid again.

To record their work in Activities 2 to 5 they can compile a table of results on copymaster 39.

Attainment target 3: Materials and their properties

Level 3	Statements of attainment	Statements of attainment
	Pupils should:	Pupils could:
	a) be able to link the use of common materials to their simple properties.	*recognise how some everyday uses of materials such as metals, plastics, wood and glass are linked to properties such as water resistance, strength, flexibility and transparency.*
	b) know that some materials occur naturally while many are made from raw materials.	*sort materials used in building into those that occur naturally, such as slate, wood, stone, and those that are manufactured, such as cement, glass and plastic.*
	c) understand some of the effects of weathering on buildings and on rocks.	*describe and recognise the signs of weathering on the stonework of older buildings and gravestones in their locality, such as discolouration, crumbling and loss of detail.*

Area of study 1	P of S 1a	LINKING PROPERTIES AND USES	C40

Purpose
To link the properties of some materials to their uses.

Materials needed
Some examples of what might be included are: rocks and pebbles; wood, wooden objects such as a bowl and a piece of carved wood, a wooden spoon and a ruler; paper of various kinds; straw and willow, e.g. used in a basket; rubber sheeting and a ball, eraser, rubber bands and a plimsoll; metals including rock containing ore, a tin can, a steel rule, watch parts and parts of a machine such as a bike or car; clay, pottery and china; clothes and linens made of natural fibres such as wool and cotton, and man-made fibres, e.g. nylon, including dishcloths and tights; glass pieces of various colours and ranging from transparent to opaque; plastic containers and extruded packaging, plastic bottles and sheeting.

Activity 1: Comparing characteristics and uses
The characteristics of materials determine their uses. For the children to begin to understand this, they need to 'match' a raw material to a 'use'. Give them objects such as a piece of rubber sheet and a ball, a log and a stool, a rock containing metal (such as iron ore) and a large bolt, and get them to do the matching. Display the resulting 'matches', and reasons for them.

Copymaster 40 can be used for the children to make their own record of the match between raw materials and uses.

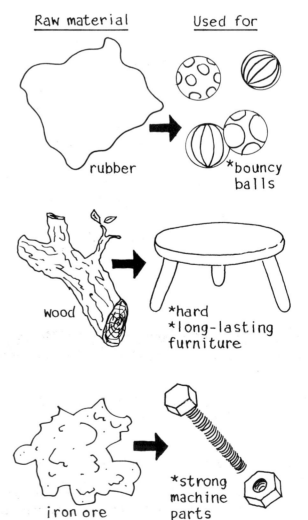

Raw material — Used for

rubber → *bouncy balls

wood → *hard *long-lasting furniture

iron ore → *strong machine parts

46

SORTING MATERIALS

 C41, 42

Purpose
To show that some materials are found naturally while others have to be made.

Materials needed
Assemble a collection of materials similar to that used at Level 2 and in Area of Study 1 on previous page.

Activity 1: What is natural and what is man-made
Give the children a range of natural and man-made materials, trying not to put in 'finished' products such as crockery or clothes (see Activity 2). Let the children sort the materials into two sets: natural and man-made. They can leave to one side the things they are not sure about. Discuss their groupings with them and help them with uncertainties.

They can record their groupings on copymaster 41.

Activity 2: Finished products using natural and other materials
Give the children a range of raw materials, samples of these materials prepared for manufacture and samples of finished products. The intention is that children should understand that man changes natural and man-made materials to produce the things we use. For example, you can include in the collection a fleece, a ball of wool and a jumper; a cotton boll, a reel of cotton thread and a skirt or tea-towel; a piece of iron ore, a metal ingot and a nut and bolt; a log, a plank and a stool; the contents of a kit for making plastic paper weights (make sure that the children do not open and handle these, as they contain harmful chemicals), plastic sheeting or shredded packaging and a comb or toothbrush; clay and a flowerpot. Let the children put these things in order from raw materials to finished product. You may then like to show them mixed products such as costume jewellery and shoes. Display the children's work. Discuss why the raw materials are so used and the reasons why, for example, we do not wear wooden vests or make wool into nuts and bolts!

The children can use copymaster 42 to record the flow from raw materials to finished products.

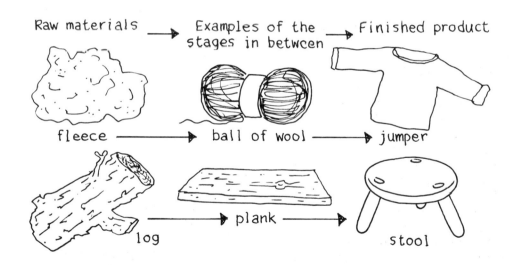

Raw materials → Examples of the stages in between → Finished product

fleece → ball of wool → jumper

log → plank → stool

WEATHERING AND ITS EFFECTS

 C43, 44

Purpose
To identify some of the effects of weathering on buildings and the landscape.

Materials needed
Clay or mud, a piece of sandstone and a bucket of water, a sink or deep tray, a small earthenware flowerpot filled with soil, pictures of different kinds of landscape, rock samples and 'matching soil', magnifiers, seedtrays, seeds such as beans or mustard and cress, scales, water jugs.

Activity 1: Effects of weather on buildings
Walk round the school buildings and the immediate neighbourhood, if possible looking at buildings built from stone, brick, corrugated iron, wood, etc. Look for signs of deterioration: cracked bricks, loose mortar, peeling paint, rotten wood, rusting iron. Discuss the

observations and the weather conditions that may, in part, have caused them. Look at the effects of rain, sun, wind and frost.

Ask the children to record their observations on copymaster 43.

Activity 2: Effects of frost

Test out how frost weathers buildings and rocks by immersing a small earth-filled flowerpot in water for several hours. The pot and soil will have absorbed all the water they can by then, and will be 'waterlogged'. This is equivalent to heavy rain. Then wrap the flowerpot in a plastic bag for hygiene and safety reasons and put it into the freezer, to create frost-like conditions. Examine the following day for signs of cracking.

Activity 3: Effects of sunshine

To show the effect of warm sunshine, make clay or mud bricks and stand them on the warmest window-sill. They will crack on drying just as the soil and mortar do in very hot conditions.

Activity 4: Weathering and the landscape

Discuss the effects of weathering on the landscape. Collect pictures of landscape features that cannot be seen in the immediate locality, e.g. rolling plains, arid land, mountains, rugged coasts, sandy shores, or look for slides or a film-strip of these. In answer to the question 'What has the weather done to this?' the children may deduce that high winds mean rough seas and cliff erosion, calm seas mean deposition of sand; cold and frost on mountain tops have weathering effects, and windy conditions take the soil away down the slope, hence infertile peaks.

Use copymaster 44 for consolidation.

Attainment target 3: Materials and their properties

Level 4	Statements of attainment	Statements of attainment
	Pupils should:	Pupils could:
	a) be able to classify materials as solids, liquids and gases on the basis of simple properties which relate to their everyday uses.	*explain why the chassis of a motor car is made from a solid material (metal), the tyres are filled with a gas (air) and a liquid fuel (petrol) is used.*
	b) know that materials from a variety of sources can be converted into new and useful products by chemical reactions.	*describe some useful everyday chemical changes, such as milk into yoghurt, wood into charcoal, and smelting ores into metals.*
	c) know that the combustion of fuel releases energy and produces waste gases.	*compare a candle and a car engine and discuss how the burning fuel transfers energy and releases gases including carbon dioxide.*
	d) know how measurements of temperature, rainfall, windspeed and direction describe the weather.	*use measurements from two contrasting periods of weather to describe the differences.*
	e) know that weathering, erosion and transport lead to the formation of sediments and different types of soil.	*describe the ways in which water, sand and ice can transport and deposit sediment, leading to soil formation.*

  | Area of study 1 | P of S 1a |

SOLIDS, LIQUIDS AND GASES

C45 –48

Purpose

To investigate some of the properties of solids, liquids and gases.

Materials needed

A collection of raw materials including: cotton thread, nylon fishing line, a ball of wool, elastic, wire in a variety of gauges ranging from fuse to garden wire, a hacksaw blade, a short length of rope of the type that may be used to support a swing, a short length of garden hose, a variety of rocks, pieces of plastic, coins, paper art straws, plastic straws and sets of gram masses; small clamps, books with pictures about architectural styles in history, bridges and building.

Also needed are salt, sugar, instant coffee, washing powder, sand, wood shavings, grated carrot (or other vegetable); glass or plastic beakers, spoons, water and timers with second hands, Celsius thermometers.

A variety of 'hard' materials in pieces suitable for putting on classroom balances, including at least two samples of similar size and shape, preferably of different metals; balances and masses; a plastic vivarium filled with water with graduations on the side, and/or plastic measuring jugs of water; a bottle of milk, an empty milk bottle, a bottle or can of fizzy drink and a similar empty bottle or can, a bottle of washing-up liquid and a similar empty bottle.

Full bottles and cans of fizzy soft drink, accurate and sensitive balance of scales.

Activity 1: Strength and shape

If possible take the children to look at a variety of buildings, noting in particular the materials used and the shapes of archways, doorways and shapes used in the construction of, for example, roofs in churches, factories, barns, railway stations. The children can also consult secondary sources such as books, photographs and film to identify the kinds of material and shape used in construction. Their research should show a pattern of the common use of triangles and curves. They can investigate further why such shapes are 'strong' ones. They can also record which materials are in common use in building construction, and why. It is possible to tie in this work with their activities in Design and Technology. There is work in AT 4 Level 5 on strength in building.

Copymaster 45 gives children the chance to identify strong shapes and draw them.

Activity 2: Strength and loads

Stronger materials do support heavier loads, and the children will already be able to predict that plastic is stronger than paper and that metals are stronger still. A test to confirm the paper–plastic comparison can be done by clamping a drinking straw made from each of these two materials in turn between two desks and suspending masses from them. Add the masses to a plastic or fabric bag, and test until the paper straw breaks or buckles permanently. If you can add one more mass to the plastic straw than could be supported by the paper straw, this will indicate that the plastic straw is stronger. The children can list some examples of the use of strong materials to carry loads, e.g. roads, bridges, girders, HGVs. Tell them that it is in fact a combination of strength and shape which enables structures to carry loads.

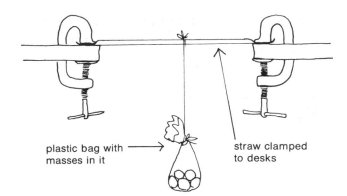

plastic bag with masses in it → straw clamped to desks

Activity 3: Hardness of different materials

Lay out a range of materials which feel 'hard', such as chalk, flint, granite, limestone, 'local' rock, slate, brick, concrete, plastic, glass, pottery, coins, metal bars. Let the children handle and inspect the samples, and then devise a strategy for systematically testing which material will make a scratch on all the others. The children should be able to find the hardest material, and rank all the others.

Their results can be tabulated on copymaster 46.

Activity 4: Playground hardness

Discuss with the children the surfaces available for them to play on at school and the surfaces they have seen in children's play areas. Discuss what it must be like to fall over on each of these surfaces, and therefore which is judged to be the hardest. The discussion may include the following list of surfaces: grass, bare earth, tarmac, concrete, bark and the special 'soft' surface which has been introduced under the equipment in some playgrounds. This work can link to an investigation of hardness and road surfacing.

Activity 5: Flexibility of different materials

A variety of materials need to be tested to see which return to their original shape when bent or stretched. The children can suspend a length of each of the following materials in turn from a clamp, the edge of the desk, or a cup hook in the wall: cotton, nylon fishing line, elastic and springs (which they can make from different kinds of wire). In each case they need to measure the length of the suspended material and mark where the end of the material comes. Masses are then put on a hanger suspended from the end in an attempt to achieve some stretch. Then the masses can be taken off and the children can note whether the material returns to its original length. The children can then list some everyday uses of elastic materials, e.g. fishing line, watch springs, washing line, curtain wire, socks.

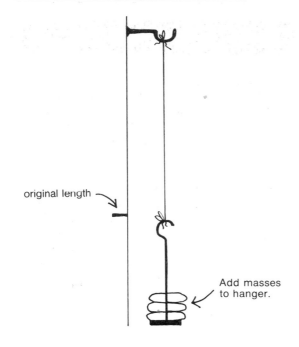

original length

Add masses to hanger.

Activity 6: New inventions

Ask the children to invent some things and to decide themselves what materials the things should be made from. They must give their reasons for the choice of material. Examples might include a flask to keep drinks hot, a roller boot, a pop-up birthday card, a carrying case for cassettes, running shoes, swimwear, a moveable toy suitable for a two-year-old.

The children can record their inventions on copymaster 47.

Activity 7: Solubility in water at room temperature

Let the children attempt to dissolve a spoonful of salt, sugar, instant coffee, washing powder, sand, wood shavings and grated carrot in different beakers of water. If they work in pairs they cannot only determine which of these materials dissolves, but also how long it takes to do so. They will need a timer with a second hand for this.

Activity 8: Solubility in hot water

Ask the children to predict what will happen to the solubility of soluble materials as the temperature of the water increases. They can repeat Activity 1 for the soluble materials, but this time they also need to record the temperature of the water. Then supply them with some warmer water and ask them to repeat the experiment. Finally, give them really hot water and get them to repeat the experiment again. Their results should show increased solubility at higher temperatures.

Discuss with the children the use we make of the fact that some solids are soluble in liquids, for example washing powder.

Copymaster 48 is intended for the children's record of these results.

Activity 9: Solids have weight and volume

To reinforce this concept the children can weigh some pieces of sample material and then, having read off the water level in a tank or jug, they can lower the sample into it and work out from the new water level the amount of water that has been displaced. Wood, polystyrene and other materials which float will have to be held beneath the surface of the water with a pencil.

Activity 10: Similar size means similar volume

Similar sized pieces, e.g. cubes or bars, of different materials will displace the same amount of water. If they are then weighed they will not weigh the same. The children can speculate on why this is so, and should be helped to understand that the difference is due to differences in density between materials.

Activity 11: Liquids have weight and volume

Weigh full and empty milk bottles, drinks cans and washing-up liquid bottles. The difference between the measurements is the weight of the liquid. Immerse the full and empty vessels in a tank of water and there will be more water displaced by the full ones. The difference in water levels will be due mostly to the liquid in the full bottle or can. Point out that this is not accurate, for even the empty containers have walls of plastic or glass, for example, which may be quite thick; even the walls of vessels have volume. Ask the children how they can determine the volume of the bottle or can. They should be able to tell from the contents printed on the container the volume of liquid inside, and work out the volume of the container itself from their figures.

Activity 12: Weighing carbon dioxide

The children can see from containers of fizzy drink that the drinks contain the gas carbon dioxide to make them fizzy. If they weigh the full containers and then take the cap or ring pull off and leave the drink to go flat they can weigh it again. The difference in 'weight' is the 'weight' of gas put into the drink.

EFFECTS OF HEATING AND COOLING

Purpose
To explain the common chain solid–liquid–gas which occurs when some materials are subjected to heat or cold.

Materials needed
Tap water, ice-cube tray, freezer, Celsius thermometers, saucers, bowls and jugs, a kettle full of water, a candle in a suitable holder and matches.

Activity 1: Effects of heat and cold on water
The children may recall a similar activity at Level 2 but now they are expected to be able to quantify the results of their experiments. The children can measure the temperature of tap water. They can pour some of this water into an ice-tray and set it to freeze in a freezer or fridge cold compartment. As ice starts to form they can take the tray out and measure the temperature again. Return the tray to the freezer. When ice-cubes have formed take the tray out and empty the ice into a bowl. The children can observe the ice melting as it returns to room temperature. They can measure the temperature periodically during the melting process. That same water, heated in the kettle, will boil, turn to steam and will recondense on cool surfaces such as the window.

Activity 2: Evaporation
A saucer of water left by an open window or on a radiator will evaporate.

You can set this up for initial observation. Then challenge the children to devise experiments to test conditions for evaporation. For example, does evaporation occur quicker in a draught, in the open air, on a day when the air pressure is high, or in warm or cold rooms. They will need to test these conditions by measuring the same amount of water out each time, and then checking their experiment every hour or so for change in water level.

Mention to the children that when they see their breath on cold mornings it is the warm water vapour from their mouths that condenses on the cold air to create the 'cloud' they see.

Activity 3: Burning a candle
Light the candle and explain to the children that the solid wax melts to a liquid which, when hot, becomes gaseous and burns giving off light, heat and smoke. The solid–liquid–gas chain is evident here.

Activity 4: Human safety and hot liquids
Tell the children that different solids become liquid and then gas at different temperatures. Warn them of the dangers of this, as boiling water scalds human skin. Cooking oil has a higher boiling-point and hot oil, as mentioned in Level 2, Area of Study 1, is therefore very dangerous indeed. There are possibilities for drama or puppet work here to produce a 'safety at home' video for the younger children in the school to watch.

Activity 5: Molecular activity
Discuss with the children what is happening at a molecular level: that all molecules in all things are in motion with kinetic energy. The molecules in solids move less than they do in liquids. When heat energy hits molecules, it is changed to kinetic energy and the molecules move even faster, sometimes sufficiently fast to cause a solid to change into a liquid (e.g. warmed ice turns to water), or a liquid into a gas.

Activity 6: Solids, liquids, gas game
The children can also play a solids, liquids, gases game, where one child thinks of a solid, liquid or gas and the others have to ask questions about its properties in order to identify it. The child being questioned can only answer 'yes' or 'no'.

Copymaster 49 gives the children the chance to link what they know about solids, liquids and gases to their uses.

USEFUL CHEMICAL CHANGE

Purpose
To show that we use chemical reactions to convert materials into products that are useful to us.

Materials needed
Plasticine® or clay, Plaster of Paris, Fimo® or other play dough; cake ingredients, mixing tools, cake cases and tins, the use of the school oven; films or videos about glass and plastic manufacture.

Activity 1: Plaster of Paris
Assemble some moulds that the children have made from clay or Plasticine®, and set them out on newspaper. Make up the Plaster of Paris as instructed. Work quickly because it begins to set within minutes. Pour the mixture into the moulds and leave until completely hard before peeling away the Plasticine® or clay. Let the children feel the vessel in which you made up the Plaster of Paris. Explain that the warmth they feel is

the sign of a chemical reaction taking place, in this case into a hard brittle material. Tell the children that the change is irreversible. Plaster of Paris is used in model making and sculpture, to embellish ceilings and mirror frames and to create a hard bandage cast round broken limbs.

Activity 2: Fimo®

Children may have handled Fimo® in *Effects of Heating and Cooling* at Level 2 (Area of Study 2, page 44). Let the children handle either Fimo® or some other soft malleable dough which, when heated in an oven, becomes irreversibly hard and brittle. All potters and some sculptors make use of this change.

Activity 3: Baking powder

Make a batch of fairy cakes using plain flour for half the batch and adding the required amount of baking powder to the other. The results using plain flour should be relatively flat, while those with baking powder in them should rise well. Explain to the children that the addition to the mixture of baking powder (which is a mixture of sodium bicarbonate and cream of tartar) allows a chemical reaction to take place during which a gas (carbon dioxide) is produced which makes the cakes rise. Here is a suggested recipe:

Caster sugar 110 g
Margarine 110 g
2 beaten eggs
Plain flour 175 g
A little water if necessary
1 level teaspoon baking powder

Cream the sugar and margarine together. Beat in the egg. Divide this mixture into two bowls. To the first add half the flour and a little water if necessary to make a dropping consistency. To the second add half the flour well mixed with the baking powder. Add water as

necessary. Spoon the mixture into cake cases in patty tins. Cook at 180°C for 15–20 minutes. The overall yield will be 14–20 cakes, and even the flat ones should be edible!

Activity 4: Glass making and plastic manufacture

Borrow a film or video which shows the process by which glass is made from, among other constituents, sand. Thus from materials of limited use we create the stuff of which our windows, doors, spectacles, drinks containers and a host of other things are made.

Look also at films about the making of various plastics to discover which involve chemical reactions among constituents in order to make products which can be used, for example, for insulation material, packaging, sheeting.

If the school is near a glass or plastics factory, or some other plant where chemical change produces useful products, ask if a manager can come along and tell the children about the manufacturing process involved.

Contact the local Higher Education Institution and ask if they have an Economic Understanding and Industrial Awareness Unit or Centre. People involved in such a Centre should be able to offer you further help and advice.

FUEL COMBUSTION

Purpose

To learn that fuel releases energy and produces waste gases.

Materials needed

Advertising brochures about gas, electric and solid fuel fires; a camping stove, saucepan, milk, mugs, spoon, drinking chocolate and a box of matches.

Activity 1: Fires

Collect some advertising brochures about gas, electric and solid fuel fires. Talk to the children about the kind of fire they have at home and how it operates. Remind them of the dangers of fire. Discuss how the fuel is burned to produce heat and waste gases which escape via a chimney or flue. The chimney is necessary both to

allow a flow of air which the fire needs to burn and also to evacuate dangerous gases from the home.

Activity 2: Camping stove

Place a camping stove at a safe distance from the children. Explain that the compressed gas inside is burned to release the heat necessary to cook on, and that waste gases escape into the air. Make the children a hot drink!

Activity 3: Matches

Look at the way a match works. The starter fuel at the tip is ignited, the wooden stick burns giving out heat, and waste gases escape. Remind the children of the dangers of matches.

Area of study 5 | **P of S 4a**

BEGINNING WEATHER RECORDS

C50, 51

Purpose
To record the weather over time, and use weather symbols.

Materials needed
Children's reference books on the weather; sugar paper, tissue paper or teacher's cut-outs (as shown in the drawing below) for masking the windows; large chalkboard and chalk or large sheet of paper and pens, selection of weather reports from the newspapers, overhead projector, video of several weather forecasts from different channels on television, thin card, scissors, felt pens, a map of the part of Britain where your school is located and light cotton pins.

Activity 1: Weather over time
Discuss the weather day by day. Get the children to observe cloud formations, estimate how long the sun shines on a particular day (e.g. most of the day, half a day) and make weather comparisons, such as whether it is cooler or warmer than yesterday.

Stick a paper border on one or more windows to direct the children's observations.

After a period of time, when the children have consulted the books, been shown signs of change in the weather and have learnt some weather names (e.g. types of clouds), they will be in a position to record some of this information. They can draw and/or write a weather picture or word each day, for about half a term, and then put them in their file.

Give the children a weather record (copymaster 50) to fill in.

Activity 2: Weather symbols
Put the children into groups. As a class, look at weather reports from the newspapers (you could use the overhead projector) and a video of weather reports. Use a large chalkboard or big sheet of paper pinned up. Ask each group in turn to give you/draw up on the board a weather symbol. Collect together like symbols according to the children's advice.

Get all the groups to allocate a different kind of weather to each member. Each child in the class then designs a new weather symbol. They can transfer their rough designs to thin card and cut out for display.

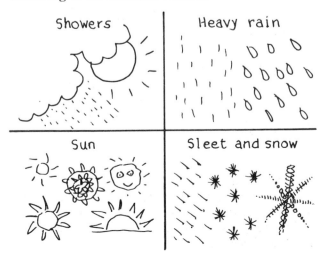

Activity 3: Weather reports and forecasts
Ask each group to compile a weather report and forecast for a different day of the week. At the end of the week collate the reports and forecasts and display these with the weather symbols. Get each group to appoint a weatherman to do a 'live broadcast'. The children can also compare their predictions about the weather with what actually happened.

The children can record their scripts on copymaster 51, and also on tape.

| Area of study 6 | P of S 4a | **MEASURING THE WEATHER** | C52 –55 |

Purpose

To show how to measure temperature and rainfall, and to explain what wind is and how to measure its speed and direction.

Materials needed

A range of different thermometers, a rain gauge and other containers in which to collect rain, plastic funnels and a bag of material pieces and fabric glue, card, balsa wood strips, nails and a toolbox for wind experiments. A hairdryer can be used as a wind machine. A windsock and wind speed indicator might be useful too.

Activity 1: Thermometers

Let the children look carefully at all the thermometers and examine the range of temperature they measure, what the liquids are inside, and what happens when they hold the bulb of the thermometer, or take it outside the classroom. Set up a Celsius room thermometer inside and a similar thermometer outside the classroom. Each day let a different child record the temperatures and put them on a class chart, alongside the temperatures predicted in the official weather forecast for the day.

A sample chart appears on copymaster 52.

Activity 2: Rainfall

With the children design an experiment to collect the rainfall over an extended period. The period you choose for this should vary according to your research on likely rainfall in your area. Use a variety of containers and let the children decide where to site the experiment safely and how to monitor collection and collation of results.

Get the children to monitor this collection and record their activities on copymaster 53.

Activity 3: Wind direction and windspeed inventions

Supply a wide range of materials. Invite the children, a small group at a time, to invent something to show either wind direction or windspeed. They can test out their inventions in class or corridor. Show them a commercially made windsock and windspeed indicator, or pictures of these, but only after they have all had a go at inventing one.

They can record work about their invention on copymaster 54.

The children can extol the virtues of their invention on copymaster 55 by writing an advertisement.

Create a display of wind information and inventions.

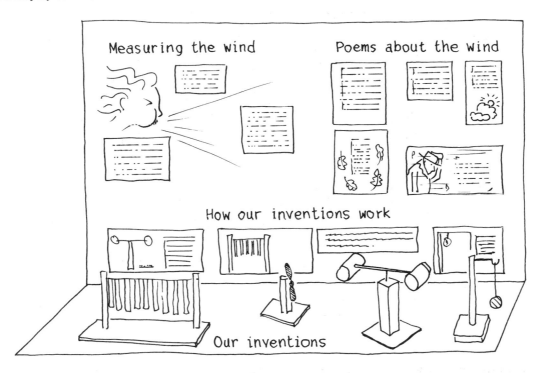

Purpose
To understand the factors producing different sediments and soils.

Materials needed
A collection of rock and soil samples of varying hue, texture, hardness and colour; magnifiers and 'dibbers'; slides, film or video showing the effects of weathering.

Activity 1: A range of rocks and soils
To open the children's discussion of this subject in detail, arrange a display of a wide variety of rocks and soil samples. Try to include some that are unfamiliar to the children. Supply magnifiers and 'dibbers' and let the children examine the samples and speculate on the kind of terrain the rocks may come from, and the likely resulting kinds of soils.

Activity 2: Effect of water, wind and ice
Discuss the effects of water, wind and ice on the landscape, including the following effects:

- Erosion and transport by seas and rivers
- Wind effects in carrying light material to new locations
- Glacial effects in the past on our landscape.

View slides or film or video showing the effects of weathering.

Activity 3: Weathering and soils
Let children examine rock and 'matching' soil specimens. Let them feel it, look at it under the magnifier, pour water into the rock and into the matching soil sample to test how porous it is (does water run through or is it absorbed?). Weigh samples of several soils (the same volume of each, perhaps that filling a small flowerpot) and compare the soils to see whether they are dense and compact or light and friable. Discuss which might be the more fertile of soils. Grow a bean, a couple of nasturtium seeds,

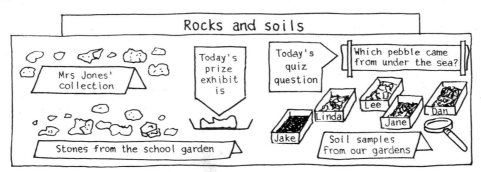

mustard and cress or sunflowers in each soil sample and note how long germination takes in each. Which turn out to be the more fertile soils? Do they have common properties described by the children in their earlier investigations?

You can use copymaster 56 to record findings (use a new sheet for each different seed grown).

Activity 4: Looking at weathering

Take the children on a trip to see parts of the local landscape where weathering, erosion and transport are occurring.

Copymaster 57 gives the children the opportunity to compile a report about the effects of water, wind and ice on the landscape.

Attainment target 3: Materials and their properties

Level 5	Statements of attainment	Statements of attainment
	Pupils should:	Pupils could:
	a) know how to separate and purify the components of mixtures using physical processes.	*select techniques such as decanting, filtration, dissolving and evaporation to separate and purify components of mixtures such as muddy or salty water.*
	b) be able to classify aqueous solutions as acidic, alkaline or neutral, using indicators.	*use natural or standard indicators to compare the acidity of drinks and solutions made from foods and soils.*
	c) understand that rusting and burning involve a reaction with oxygen.	*explain how the processes of rusting and burning can be slowed by reducing contact with oxygen.*
	d) understand the water cycle in terms of the physical processes involved.	*use knowledge of heating, evaporation, condensation, movements in the atmosphere and flow of water at the Earth's surface, to explain the water cycle.*

Area of study 1	P of S 1e	

SEPARATING AND PURIFYING A MIXTURE

Purpose
To explain and implement various techniques for separating and purifying mixtures.

Materials needed
Sand, salt, iron filings, beakers, a funnel, filter-paper and a magnet covered in paper; several different inks or black felt-tip pens; blotting paper.

Activity 1: Separating a mixture of sand, salt and iron filings
Give the children the dry mixture and challenge them to separate out the three things. They may decide to add water right away to dissolve the salt. Then they can filter off the salt solution, dry the filter paper, draw off the iron filings with the covered magnet and set them aside (make sure the magnet is covered or the iron filings will be stuck there forever). The sand can be shaken off the dry filter-paper. If the salt solution is left to evaporate, the salt will be left in the beaker.

Alternatively, the iron filings can be drawn off with the magnet right at the beginning of the experiment if water has not yet been added at that stage.

Activity 2: Purification
Discuss with the children the implications of their experiment in Activity 1 for the processes involved in purifying drinking water and sewage and cleaning swimming pools. Relate this work to their study of pollution in AT2.

Activity 3: 'Who dun it?'
This one is for fun! Out of sight of the children, write a note of confession about a bogus crime. Use a sample of black ink or a black felt-tip, and blot it with blotting paper, making sure there are substantial blots of ink. Create a number of imaginary characters who may have committed the crime (rather like the people in the game of Cludeo®). Assign each character a different

black ink or felt-tip pen. Let the children mark strips of blotting paper with the inks and set the strips into jars with a little water in them, so that the inky end dips into the water. Anchor each strip to the side of the jar using a peg so that the strip does not flop right down

inside the jar. The constituent colours in the inks should separate up the blotting strips, and only one will match the colour array that can be obtained from the blots made by the ink used in writing the confession note.

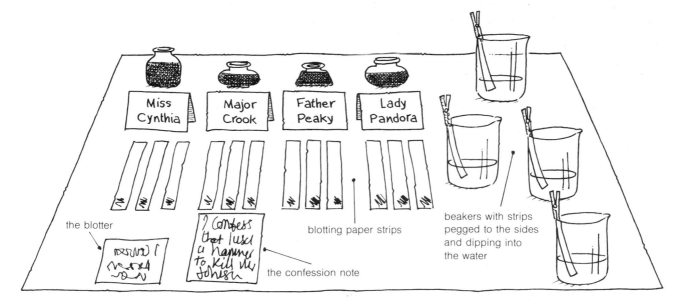

the blotter

the confession note

blotting paper strips

beakers with strips pegged to the sides and dipping into the water

---

CLASSIFYING SOLUTIONS

C58

Purpose
To be able to use indicators to determine whether aqueous solutions are acidic, alkaline or neutral.

Materials needed
A red cabbage, boiling distilled water, bowl, strainer, jar; a variety of aqueous solutions including, for example, lemon juice, squash, orange juice, peat in water, soap in water, washing powder solution, chalk in water, salt solution; litmus paper and the more sensitive universal indicator which has a colour range (similar to those found in soil-testing kits), transparent containers for the solutions.

Activity 1: Red cabbage test
Cut up the red cabbage, into a bowl. Pour on about half a litre of boiling distilled water. Leave the mixture until the water is very cool. Strain the liquid and throw away the cabbage. Test a variety of solutions using a

little of the cabbage water as indicator. Acid will turn it red, alkali green.

Activity 2: The litmus test
Dip litmus paper into a variety of solutions and record whether each solution is acid (litmus pink) or alkali (litmus blue).

Activity 3: Universal indicator
Test each solution again using the more sensitive indicator. The children can record the colour shown on the indicator and the degree of acidity or alkalinity of the solution.

The children's results can be recorded and tabulated on copymaster 58.

RUSTING AND BURNING

Purpose
To show we need oxygen for things to rust or burn.

Materials needed
A viewing of metal parts on the school building, a car or bicycle; four iron nails, a jar of water, Vaseline® or grease; a candle and holder, matches, glass jar; a visiting fire-fighter.

Activity 1: Looking for rust
Let the children look for rust. Some things they may look at include the following:

- The bodywork on a car that is some years old
- A bike
- Door hinges, railings and other metal parts on the outside of the school buildings.

They need to locate where the rust occurs most. Discuss their findings, and explain that iron needs oxygen from the air and moisture to rust. We prevent that process by excluding the air and water from the surface of the metal with a 'coating' like chrome or paint. The children will have seen what happens when the surface coating becomes chipped or flakes off.

Activity 2: A rusting experiment
Put a large iron nail into a glass jar with water in it. Cover a second nail in a thick layer of grease (Vaseline® works well) and add this to the jar. Leave the jar for some time – allow several weeks.

Alongside the jar set down two nails in air, the first as it is and the second coated with grease.

After some time the children should note that the nails covered in grease should be rust-free or have little rust while the others should show signs of rust. Rusting requires oxygen from the air and moisture, and if these are excluded from iron it will not rust.

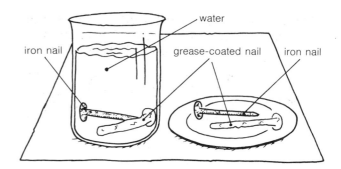

Activity 3: Burning needs oxygen
Light a candle and set it safely upright in a holder. Invert a glass jar over it and watch the candle go out for lack of a supply of oxygen from the air. Do observe safety regulations in doing this experiment.

Activity 4: Excluding oxygen to put out a fire
Invite a local fire-fighter to visit the school and discuss why foam is used in fire extinguishers to put out fires.

THE WATER CYCLE

C59

Purpose
To explain the water cycle.

Materials needed
Children's reference books on water; thick card, two circular templates, paper-fasteners, scissors, saucers, graduated cylinders, water.

Activity 1: The water cycle
Explain to the children, and research with them in the appropriate books, the water cycle and its circularity. It includes the following steps: water in rivers reaching sea, air warmed over land rises drawing in 'wind' over sea which picks up water vapour; water vapour in air carried over land, warmed by land and then rises. It then cools and water vapour condenses and falls as rain, rain runs into ground and re-emerges as a spring; the spring trickle becomes a stream and then a river, the river runs down to the sea. The children can record this on a water cycle wheel.

The children can construct their own wheels using the instructions given on copymaster 59.

Activity 2: Evaporation and condensation
The children can demonstrate these by putting a small quantity of water into a container with a wide top, such as washing-up bowl, and enclosing the bowl in a tent made from clear polythene, complete with a central pole made from, say, a bean stick in a pot of soil. This will need to be rigged on a bench near a window where it will receive direct sunlight. The water in the bowl will evaporate and condense on the polythene. The condensed water can be collected at the edge of the polythene tent. This is a form of water 'still' similar to apparatus used to distil liquids. Some children may like to find out more about such devices in relation to survival in desert conditions.

LANDSCAPE FORMATION

Purpose
To explain simply how landscapes are formed.

Materials needed
Corrugated card pieces, strips of coloured card and Plasticine®; children's reference books, world map.

Activity 1: Earthquakes and volcanoes around the world
Discuss earth movements, earthquakes and volcanoes. Research these in the appropriate books. Pin up a world map. As the children discover the locations of volcanoes and areas of earthquake activity through their research they can tag these using pins and stickers on the world map. Some discussion will arise about patterns that start to emerge.

Activity 2: Internal processes
Arrange $10 \text{ cm} \times \frac{1}{2}$ m strips of corrugated card on top of one another on a desk. Push the short edges of the strips towards the middle and observe what happens. The layers will fold, and the height and number of folds

will depend on the speed and severity of 'push'. If the strips are then placed between two tables and pressure is applied underneath, the card will buckle and tear.

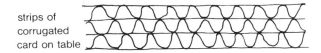

strips of corrugated card on table

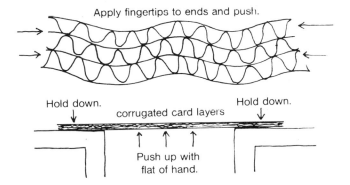

Apply fingertips to ends and push.

Hold down.   Hold down.
corrugated card layers
Push up with
flat of hand.

You can try the same activities with strips of coloured card sandwiched between layers of Plasticine®.

Do tell the children that there are many forces at work in landscape formation. While pressure beneath the Earth's crust may contribute to earthquakes and the eruption of molten lava and gas, there are also slow movements of parts of the crust alongside each other, which sometimes cause a kind of 'rubbing' which also, at times, has sudden earthquake-like effects on the landscape.

Activity 3: Weathering
Remind the children of their work at Level 4 (see Area of Study 7 *Rocks and soils* page 55). Take the children to suitable local sites or on a field trip so that they may observe and investigate weathering in the landscape. It may be possible to visit one or two of these:

- A river eroding its banks
- The seashore, to observe the action of the sea
- Hill tops subject to wind and rain erosion
- Exposed land where frost has affected the ground.

ATTAINMENT TARGET 4: Physical processes

Pupils should develop knowledge and understanding of:

i electricity and magnetism;

ii energy resources and energy transfer;

iii forces and their effects;

iv light and sound;

v the Earth's place in the Universe.

Programme of study (relating to attainment target 4)

1a Pupils should have the opportunity to construct simple circuits.

1b They should investigate the effects of using different components, of varying the flow of electricity in a circuit and the heating and magnetic effects. They should plan and record construction details of a circuit using drawings and diagrams.

Level 3	A/S 2	page 72
Level 3	A/S 3	page 73
Level 4	A/S 1	page 81
Level 4	A/S 2	page 82
Level 5	A/S 1	page 91
Level 5	A/S 2	page 92

1c They should learn about the dangers associated with the use of mains electricity and appropriate safety measures.

Level 3	A/S 1	page 71

1d They should investigate the properties of magnetic and non-magnetic materials.

Level 2	A/S 1	page 63
Level 2	A/S 2	page 64

1e They should begin to explore simple circuits for sensing, switching and control, including the use of logic gates.

Level 5	A/S 3	page 93
Level 5	A/S 4	page 94

2a Pupils should investigate movement using a variety of devices, for example *toys and models*, which are self-propelled or driven and use motors, belts, levers and gears.

Level 4	A/S 4	page 83

2b They should investigate changes that occur when familiar substances are heated and cooled, and the concepts of 'hot' and 'cold' in relation to their body temperature.

Level 2	A/S 3	page 64
Level 2	A/S 4	page 65

2c They should survey, including the use of secondary sources, the range of fuels used in the home and at school, their efficient use and their origins.

Level 3	A/S 4	page 73
Level 5	A/S 8	page 96

2d They should be introduced to the idea that energy sources may be renewable or non-renewable and consider the implications of limited global energy resources.

Level 5	A/S 5	page 94
Level 5	A/S 7	page 95

2e They should be introduced to the idea of energy transfer.

Level 4	A/S 3	page 82
Level 4	A/S 4	page 83
Level 5	A/S 6	page 95

3a Pupils should explore different types of forces including gravity and use measurements to compare their effects in, for example, *moving things and bridge building*. They should investigate the strength of a simple structure.

Level 2	A/S 5	page 66
Level 2	A/S 6	page 67
Level 2	A/S 7	page 67
Level 4	A/S 5	page 84
Level 4	A/S 7	page 86

3b They should be introduced to the idea that forces act in opposition to each other, that one force may be bigger than another, or equal to it, and that the relative sizes and directions of the forces can affect the movement of an object.

Level 3	A/S 5	page 74
Level 3	A/S 6	page 74
Level 4	A/S 6	page 84
Level 5	A/S 9	page 97
Level 5	A/S 10	page 98

3c They should investigate the factors involved in floating and sinking.

Level 4	A/S 6	page 84

3d They should explore friction and investigate the ways in which the speed of a moving object can be changed by the application of forces. This work should be set in everyday situations, for example, *road safety, transport (including cycling and sailing), balancing systems and hydraulic mechanisms in model making*.

Level 4	A/S 8	page 87
Level 5	A/S 11	page 99

4a Pupils should learn that sounds are heard because they travel to the ear and that they can do so via a variety of materials.

Level 3	A/S 10	page 77
Level 3	A/S 11	page 77

4b They should learn that sounds are made when objects vibrate, and investigate how sounds are changed in pitch, loudness and timbre, by changing the characteristics of the vibrating objects, for example *by changing length, tension, thickness of material of the vibrating object or the way it is made to vibrate, as exemplified by using musical instruments*.

Level 5	A/S 14	page 101
Level 5	A/S 15	page 103
Level 5	A/S 16–17	page 103

4c They should be aware of the obtrusive nature of some sounds in the environment.

Level 5	A/S 18	page 104

4d They should learn about the reflection of both light and sound and relate this to everyday effects (mirrors, echoes).

Level 3	A/S 7	page 75
Level 3	A/S 8	page 75
Level 3	A/S 9	page 76
Level 3	A/S 12	page 78
Level 5	A/S 12	page 100
Level 5	A/S 13	page 100

4e They should learn that light travels faster than sound by considering natural events such as thunderstorms.

Level 4	A/S 9	page 87

4f They should explore the effects produced by shining light through such objects as *lenses, colour filters, water, prisms*.

Level 2	A/S 8	page 68
Level 3	A/S 7	page 75
Level 5	A/S 12	page 100
Level 5	A/S 13	page 100

4g They should also investigate the formation of shadows and represent in drawings their ideas about how light varies in terms of brightness, colour and shade.

Level 2	A/S 8	page 68
Level 2	A/S 9	page 70

5a Pupils should track the path of the Sun using safe procedures such as a shadow stick or sundial.

Level 4	A/S 12	page 89

5b They should study, using direct observations where possible, the night sky including the position and appearance of bright planets and the Moon.

Level 3	A/S 13	page 100
Level 5	A/S 20	page 105

5c They should learn about the motions of the Earth, Moon and Sun in order to explain day and night, day length, year length, phases of the Moon, eclipses and the seasons. They should be introduced to the order and general movements of the planets around the Sun.

Level 2	A/S 10	page 70
Level 3	A/S 13	page 79
Level 3	A/S 14	page 79
Level 4	A/S 10	page 88
Level 4	A/S 11	page 88
Level 4	A/S 12	page 89
Level 4	A/S 13	page 90
Level 5	A/S 19	page 105

62

Attainment target 4: Physical processes

Level 2	Statements of attainment	Statements of attainment
	Pupils should:	Pupils could:

Statements of attainment

Pupils should:

a) know that magnets attract some materials and not others and can repel each other.

b) understand the meaning of hot and cold relative to the temperature of their own bodies.

c) understand that pushes and pulls can make things start moving, speed up, slow down or stop.

d) know that light passes through some materials and that when it does not shadows may be formed.

e) know that the Earth, Sun and Moon are separate spherical bodies.

Statements of attainment

Pupils could:

show how a magnet can be used as a means to sort objects and how repulsion between two magnets can be used to propel a simple toy vehicle.

determine whether hot and cold tap water are warmer or cooler than themselves by feeling them and using a thermometer.

show and explain, using moving toys, how pushes and pulls can start or stop motion and also affect how fast things move.

explain that a light source needs to be blocked in a controlled way for finger shadows to be made.

be asked to imagine they are on a spacecraft looking out of the windows and draw the Earth, Sun and Moon as they would see them from space.

Area of study 1	P of S 1d	**MAGNETS ATTRACT SOME MATERIALS**	C60

Purpose
To show that magnets attract some materials and not others.

Materials needed
A collection of small pieces of various materials, including paper, a candle, brass, a can, steel, iron, glass, cork, rubber, plastic and wood. Objects such as paper clips, drawing pins, buttons (brass, other metal and plastic). Bar, horseshoe and circular magnets.

Activity 1: What does a magnet attract?
Arrange a display of magnets and small items made of a variety of materials. Let the children experiment to find out what is attracted to the magnet. When the materials have been sorted into two sets, the children can suggest what is similar about all those things which are attracted to the magnet. They will note that all the things the magnet has attracted are metal, but that not all metal objects are attracted to it. Tell them that iron has to be present for attraction to occur.

The children will want to experiment on objects around the room and on buttons, eyelets, jewellery and other things they are wearing. Tell them that magnets should be kept AWAY from wrist-watches, clocks, cassettes and videos because they can disrupt the working of these.

Activity 2
The children can carry their exploration further by finding out whether magnets still attract through the table, through glass or plastic. They can also begin to experiment with the strength of magnets by seeing how many paper clips each of a variety of magnets will pick up.

The children can consolidate work on magnetic attraction on copymaster 60.

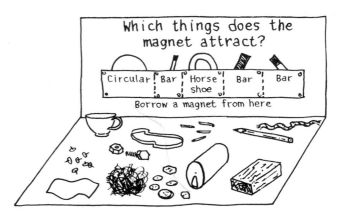

Which things does the magnet attract?

Circular	Bar	Horse shoe	Bar	Bar

Borrow a magnet from here

MAGNETIC NORTH AND SOUTH

Purpose
To explain the Earth's magnetic field, and the fact that magnets can repel one another.

Materials needed
Bar magnet, a clamp on a stand, string, chalk, a pocket compass.

Activity 1: Magnetic north and south
Tie a piece of string around the magnet and suspend it from the clamp so that it can swing freely. If it is difficult to balance the magnet, make a pipe-cleaner cradle for it. The magnet will come to rest lying in a north-south direction. Lay a piece of paper under the magnet. Draw round the paper with a piece of chalk, carefully marking one corner, and draw a line to mark exactly how the magnet was at rest. Move the suspended magnet right away and show the children a pocket compass. They may know what it is and what it is used for. You can show the children that if you align the pointer in a north-south direction it should match the direction of 'lie' of the suspended magnet. Tell the children that the earth is like an enormous magnet. If we allow a small magnet to move around, it will line up with the earth's magnetic north and south. Let the children take a compass outside the classroom and also into the playground. Then discuss with them the constancy of north.

Activity 2: Using a compass
Lay out a map, preferably of the area surrounding the school. It should have a geographic north printed on it. If you set the compass down on the map, the children should be able to turn the map so that north on the map corresponds to north on the compass. This is just how walkers, orienteers and other travellers work out their route.

Use copymaster 61 for children to record which is north on a 'map' of the classroom. They will need help with this.

Activity 3: Magnets can repel each other
Suspend a bar magnet as in Activity 1, and bring one end of another bar magnet near to one end of it. One end of the hand-held magnet will attract, the other will repel the pole of the hanging magnet. Tell the children that like poles repel one another. See if you can buy some small magnetic toys. These can be made to swivel away from one another.

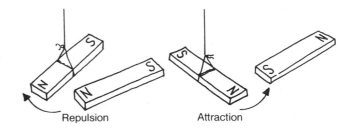

Repulsion   Attraction

FEELING HOT AND COLD

Purpose
To explain the maintenance of body temperature and what is happening when we feel hot or cold.

Materials needed
Plastic beakers, scraps of different types of material.

Activity 1: Keeping warm
Tell the children that to be healthy and to work properly our bodies must not be too hot or too cold but at just the right temperature. Heat energy keeps our bodies warm and it is converted from the chemical energy in the food we eat. We help our bodies to stay warm by insulating them with clothes.

With the children, look at their outdoor clothes on a cool day. Contrast what we need to wear outdoors on a winter's day compared with a summer's day to keep our bodies at the right temperature.

Let each child draw him/herself wearing winter and summer clothes on copymaster 62.

Activity 2: Temperature and exercise
Use a PE lesson. Get the children to say how they feel at the start of the lesson. Do some strenuous and active floorwork. Then ask them to say how they are feeling. They may say things like 'hot', 'tired' or 'hungry'. Explain that the chemical energy in the food they have eaten is being changed into two other sorts of energy: kinetic (movement) energy and heat energy.

Activity 3: Heat insulation
Discuss the idea that clothing keeps us warm, as in Activity 1, and cool, as when doing PE (Activity 2). Then set up an experiment to find out the kinds of materials which will keep in heat energy and those which allow heat energy loss. Wrap similar plastic beakers or bottles containing hot water in various

kinds of material including wool, cotton, plastic, paper and nylon. Feel each container periodically to check which one seems to be cooling down quickest.

The children can record this experiment on copymaster 63.

Set up a display of clothes we wear and the results of Activity 3.

| Area of study 4 | P of S 2c | **TEMPERATURE** | C64, 65 |

Purpose
To establish that temperature is a measure of hot or cold.

Materials needed
Hot and cold water, two beakers and a bowl; temperature indicator strips, Celsius thermometer with easily visible column, a maximum and minimum thermometer, a clinical thermometer; a variety of cups and beakers and a large jug containing a hot drink.

Activity 1: Human judgement and temperature
Put hot water into one beaker, cold into the other and warm water into the bowl. Let the children, each in turn, put one hand into the hot water, the other into the cold and then both into the warm water. They should find that the warm water feels cold on the hand that has been in hot, and hot on the hand that has been in cold. Tell the children that this shows that we are not always good at judging heat and cold. We need instruments to help us.

Activity 2: Temperature indicators
Show the children a temperature indicator strip, suitable for use in finding out whether a small child is running a temperature, meaning that he/she is unwell. Show the children what it does and try it out.

Activity 3: Thermometers
Let the children see and handle a Celsius thermometer. Ask them what it is for. Tell them that when the liquid in the bulb gets warmer, the liquid expands. The only space it can move to is the stem of the thermometer, so up it goes. Then let them see a maximum and minimum thermometer. Discuss where these may be useful, including greenhouses and weather stations. Finally, show them a clinical thermometer, noting that the scale is different and that there is a kink in the stem. The children can draw and label the thermometers, and explain why the scales and/or ranges of temperature vary.

Activity 4: Measuring air temperature
Show the children how to read a thermometer, with the indicating level at eye level. Let them investigate temperature change at school, controlling some of the variables. For example, they may use a fixed site, or a certain height above ground; they may record only indoors or only outside. It may be a good idea to place a number of thermometers around the school, and at fixed times let the children go off and read them.

The children can write down their efforts on copymaster 64.

Activity 5: Measuring the temperature of liquids
Let the children try to discover what shape of cup keeps a drink hot the longest by pouring a hot drink into a number of cups, mugs and beakers. The temperature of the drink must then be taken at regular intervals. You may also discuss the relevance of the material the cups and mugs are made of.

Results from this experiment can be recorded on copymaster 65.

Activity 6: Heating raises temperature and cooling lowers it
The children know this! But to prove it, they can take the temperature of some water or milk and then, under supervision, heat the liquid in a pan. The temperature of the liquid can be read every couple of minutes. They can then reverse the experiment, going below room temperature by putting the liquid in the fridge.

Activity 7: Heat can cause expansion, cooling contraction
Discuss examples of this in the children's experience: hot feet may mean shoes feel tight, cakes come out of

65

the tin more easily if left to cool slightly first. Then demonstrate these phenomena by making popcorn and looking at, for example, custard which has been allowed to go cold: the level of the hot custard can be seen on the side of the jug, above the present 'cold level'. (Note that water turning to ice is a notable exception to the rule.) If the school has a bar breaker now is the time to use it.

Activity 8: Heat-sensitive equipment

Discuss the fact that the fire service and other emergency services sometimes need to use heat sensitive 'cameras' to detect whether anyone is trapped in collapsed buildings. The camera is sensitive to the heat energy given out by the live human being.

PUSH AND PULL IN SPORTS AND GAMES

Purpose
To show that human pushes and pulls make things start to move, go faster, swerve and stop in sports and games.

Materials needed
Equipment used in a variety of games and sports, including, e.g. roller boots, skateboard, ice-skates, skipping-ropes, football, table tennis bat, a bicycle, sledge, a video of snippets of various sports in action, or a range of sports pictures, a smooth board and some coins for 'shove ha'penny', marbles, coffee jar lids and round cheese box lids, and models and toys with wheels.

Activity 1: Push and pull in active sport
Let the children examine and discuss a range of items used in active sport and talk about where the pushes and pulls occur and what it is that moves in a rugby scrum, in a kick-off, on a bicycle or on roller boots, for example. Let the children try out or use school equipment to help them to determine where they are pushing and pulling and what it is that moves. Create a display of sports items and pictures of sports in action. The children can add their own labelled drawings of people playing sport, marking in the push and pull and movement.

Copymaster 66 can be used by the children for work on the idea of human muscle power giving the push and pull in sport. There are complex ideas here, and human movements are not always simple enough to carry a straightforward 'push' or 'pull' label. Discuss this with the children to clarify their thinking.

Activity 2: Pull and push demonstrations
Let each child practise skipping using a rope. They can skip and determine when they are pulling, when they are pushing and what moves as a result of those forces.

Activity 3: Push and pull with games and toys
A 'shove ha'penny' board is ideal for showing push. Create one on a polished wood or plastic worktop surface (e.g. Formica®), with spaces marked on it as shown (see below). Place this flat on the table.

A coin is placed so that it slightly overlaps the starting edge of the board. The children apply force ('shove') directly to the coin with the flat or heel of the hand to get it to move. The aim of the game is to get three coins in each of the nine spaces on the board. To have a turn you shove five coins.

Toys on wheels, including Lego® models, toy cars, prams and pushchairs all give children the chance to apply direct force in moving something, accelerating it, swerving it and stopping it. If the children trap some marbles under the lid of a jar, they have an experimental toy that responds very well to push and pull.

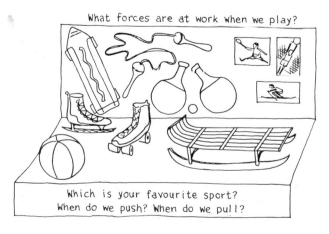

What forces are at work when we play?

Which is your favourite sport? When do we push? When do we pull?

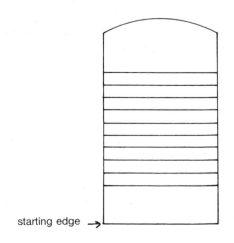

starting edge →

PUSH AND PULL IN USE OF TOOLS

Purpose
To demonstrate that human push and pull can operate hand tools.

Materials needed
Wood offcuts, large nails, a hammer, a saw, a hoist (like that available with some washing-lines) or clothes' airer; wire coat-hanger, cotton reel, plastic straw, weight, piece of string. These are the minimum tools necessary, but ideally every child should have a chance to experiment with a range of tools, under adult guidance and supervision.

Activity 1: Force in using a hammer
Bang in a nail. This uses push. Human force, applied through the hammer has made the nail move.

Activity 2: Force in using a saw
In closely supervised conditions let the children saw through a piece of wood. Let them determine whether they are applying as much force on the pull as the push stroke.

Activity 3: Pulleys
Ask the children to look for pulleys in use on building sites. Demonstrate the use of a pulley in helping human force using a washing-line hoist or a clothes' airer. Let the children try it out. Then help the children

make a single fixed pulley by first cutting the straight part off a wire coat-hanger. Insert the cut ends through a cotton reel which has a length of plastic straw inserted through the centre. Suspend the pulley and dangle a weight on a piece of string over the reel. Heave-ho! Human pull is doing the work. Does the pulley make pulling more comfortable? A simple pulley does not give mechanical advantage, but does make work more convenient.

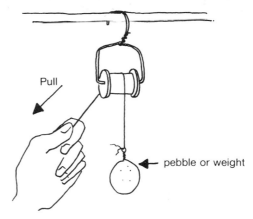

Use copymaster 67 for the children to indicate whether a range of hand tools use push or pull forces.

AIR AND WATER PUSH AND PULL

Purpose
To show that liquids and gases can exert force and that we make use of these forces.

Materials needed
Pictures of a hydroelectric power station, windmills, windsock, windvane and signs above shops and on garage forecourts; a model sailboat and a blow football set. Pictures of and information about watermills, a toy water-wheel, an empty drinks can, pieces of balsa wood and card, plastic drinking straws, strong model glue. Access to a tap and sink.

Activity 1: Air push
Look at a range of pictures with the children, including windmills, windsocks, windvanes and hanging and free-standing signs. Discuss what happens to these in light breeze and strong wind.

Activity 2: Air push and sailboats
A small sailboat in a sink can be made to move and turn by creating a 'wind'. A piece of card flapped up and

down will create a breeze, or the children can blow on the sail. They can determine what it is about the force ('wind') that affects the boat. Speed and direction are two factors involved. They can experiment with card pieces and tubes and drinking straws to change the direction and 'force' of the blow.

Activity 3: Blow football
Play the game and discuss the direction of the push given by the air and the direction of subsequent movement of the ball.

Activity 4: Uses of water force
Look at the working of a watermill. The water 'push' on the wheel turns the machinery in the mill to grind the corn.

Show pictures of a hydroelectric power station and explain briefly that it is the force of the flowing water that is used to make electricity.

Activity 5: To show water force

You may have a water-wheel bought for sand and water play. If so, the children can find out what makes it go round quicker. Is it more water, or the distance the water falls onto the wheel?

Make a water-wheel from an empty drinks can with stiff card flaps stuck to it. Give the wheel a pencil or plastic straw axle and suspend it under a running tap. Make sure the sink cannot be plugged! Let the children see what happens when just a trickle of water falls on the wheel, and then when the tap is turned on full.

SEE-THROUGH AND OPAQUE MATERIALS

Purpose

To show that light goes through some things, and forms shadow when it does not.

Materials needed

Pieces of glass, plastic sheet, coloured cellophane® sweet wrappers or filters, lenses from old spectacles and sun-glasses, glass blocks and prisms, and containers with water in them; an overhead projector and some opaque objects with distinctive outline; torches, a sheet screen, shadow puppet making materials, including paper, card, glue, scissors, pea sticks, a craft knife and sticky tape; photographic paper, a black changing bag, sheets of clear, rigid plastic (A4 size), tray of fixer, tray of water.

Activity 1: Seeing through objects

Let the children think of all the things there are that they can see through. Let them play with glass pieces (with protected edges), pieces of plastic, smoked and coloured filters, lenses, glass blocks and prisms and containers with water in them. Tell the children that they can see through all these things because the light we see by comes through them.

Activity 2: Shadow-making 1

Darken the classroom and shine a torch on the wall. Ask a child to stand between the torch and the wall. The children will be able to see the resulting shadow, and suggest why it should occur. The children can try making animal-shaped shadows.

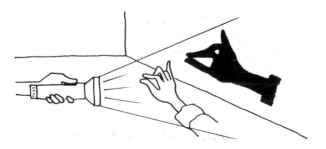

Activity 3: Shadow-making 2

Set up an overhead projector to shine on a screen or wall. Place an everyday object on the projector and its shadow will be projected. Discuss what is happening.

Activity 4: Shadow puppets

Make some shadow puppets from card and paper. Set up a home-made screen from a sheet, as shown here.

It is best if the screen slopes forward a little, for the puppets can then be leant against the screen when they are on stage but not moving. Create and perform a show for the whole class, or an assembly.

The children can record their work on shadow puppets on copymaster 68.

Activity 5: Light-sensitive materials

Put a box of photographic paper into a changing bag which you can make from light excluding fabric or buy from a photographic dealer. A design for one is shown below and overleaf.

Let the children lay some shapes like leaves and grasses on an ordinary sheet of paper to make a pattern. Put your hands into the bag and get out a sheet of paper from the box. Close the box. Let the children transfer their pattern from the ordinary paper to the sheet of photographic paper. Put a sheet of clear, rigid plastic on top to hold the pattern of leaves and grasses

still. Take the photographic paper outside and put in the sunshine until the paper turns a deep colour. This will take from fifteen seconds to thirty minutes depending on the strength of the Sun. Take off the pattern-making materials and submerge the paper in a tray of fixer. Follow the timing instructions that come with the fixer. Put the paper into a tray of water. Wash under running water after the lesson. Leave to dry naturally. The children can produce stunning 'shadow pictures' like this, since the paper lying under the objects remains unexposed.

Pattern for changing bag

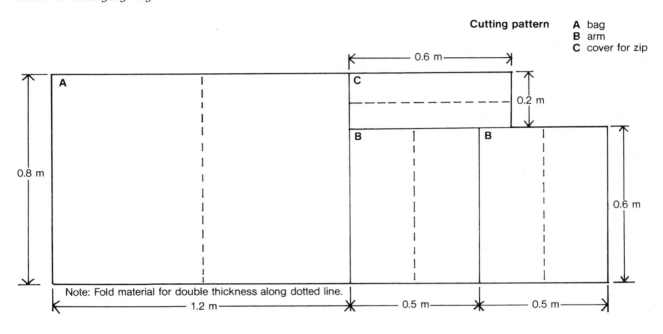

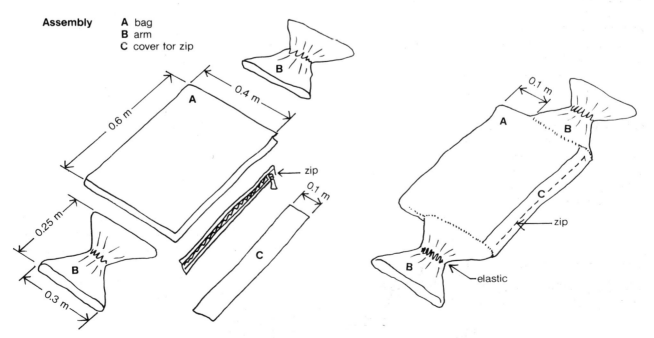

Source: *Classroom Photography* by Carol Colledge (Ilford, June 1984)

LIGHT, COLOUR AND SHADE

Purpose
To draw light, colour and shade.

Materials needed
As wide a range of drawing materials and surfaces to draw on as you can muster, including pencils, charcoal, chalks, pastels, pens, felt tips and newsprint, cartridge paper, sugar paper, chalkboards; black and white and colour photographs; a camera and film.

Activity 1: Drawing
Give the children opportunities and time to experiment with all the drawing materials to depict light and shade in their pictures. When there are strong shadows in and around the classroom point them out to the children, and let them have a good look at what happens to colours and shapes when they are in deep shadow.

Activity 2: Looking at photographs
Display a selection of photographs which show light and shade. Black and white pictures are particularly good because the colour does not distract the eye from the light and shade. The children could try representing the shadows they can see in these pictures using other drawing materials.

Activity 3: Taking photographs
You or the children can take photographs in and around the school, to show light and shade. Tell them that taking photographs is like drawing with the eye!

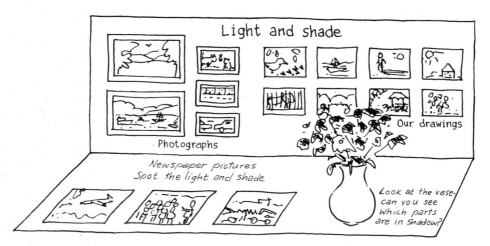

EARTH, SUN AND MOON

Purpose
To learn that the Earth, Sun and Moon are separate spherical bodies.

Materials needed
Videos of weather forecasts, appropriate computer software, books and charts about the Earth, Sun and Moon; an orrery.

Activity 1: The Earth
Look at videos of weather forecasts showing satellite pictures of the earth and computer software pictures of the Earth. Search books for photographs of the Earth taken from space. Have a good look at all the pictures and discuss what the Earth looks like.

Activity 2: Our location on planet Earth
Just for fun, let the children work out their own address, or the school address, taking it up to the postcode. Then add extra lines recording Country . . . UK, Europe, Planet . . . Earth, The universe. Address a giant envelope for display.

Class 7a
Hazelwood County Primary School
Treesville
Leafshire ZZ1 2YX
England
U.K.
Planet Earth

Our Full Address

Activity 3: The Sun and Moon
Look at books and charts to find pictures of the Sun and Moon and talk about your findings. Details of American and Russian space trips will yield photographs of the Moon and its surface.

Borrow an orrery and show the children the relative positions, size and motions of the Earth, Sun and Moon.

Copymaster 69 is a worksheet on which the children can record some Earth, Sun and Moon facts. Tell the children that the outlines are not drawn to scale.

Attainment target 4: Physical processes

Level 3	**Statements of attainment**	**Statements of attainment**
	Pupils should:	Pupils could:
	a) know that a complete circuit is needed for electrical devices to work.	*build simple circuits including switches, bulbs and buzzers.*
	b) know that there is a range of fuels used in the home.	*make a list of the different fuels that can be used for heating and cooking at home.*
	c) understand that forces can affect the position, movement and shape of an object.	*explain how the shape and movement of a sponge ball change when it is hit with a bat.*
	d) know that light and sound can be reflected.	*use a mirror to illuminate a dark space in a model; explain that an echo is caused by sound bouncing off the walls of a tunnel, cliff or building*
	e) know that the appearance of the Moon and the altitude of the Sun change in a regular and predictable manner.	*describe their records of the appearance of the Moon over a period of a month and of the path of the Sun over two separate days that were several months apart.*

 Area of study 1 | P of S 1c | # ELECTRICITY: DANGERS AND SAFETY

Purpose
To show that electricity can be dangerous, and to know what to do to be safe.

Materials needed
Books and publicity material related to the dangers of electricity and the correct use of home appliances; photographs of lightning.

Activity 1: Hazards at home
Look at the books and leaflets with the children and discuss the hazards of electricity at home, including trailing flex, electricity points accessible to small children, water near appliances. Let the children check their homes JUST BY LOOKING, and report back to their parents and teachers on the possible sources of hazard.

The children can complete copymaster 70 to record some of these hazards.

Activity 2: Hazards at school
Groups of children, accompanied by an adult, can tour the school looking for sources of electrical hazard; e.g. are sockets loose, plugs ill-fitting, flexes on appliances worn? Are there appliances near water (e.g. the kettle on the staffroom draining board)? They should draw or write where there are hazards, and report orally to the headteacher.

Activity 3: Hazards in the kitchen
The school cook may be able to talk to the children about all the care he/she has to take with electricity.

He/she may be able to point out the sources of danger in the school kitchen while showing the children round.

Activity 4: Static electricity

Discuss with the children the sensation of a shock from the static in vigorously brushed hair, nylon petticoats and some jumpers. Explain that lightning is electricity which sometimes creates sparks and can set fire to trees.

Activity 5: Danger logos

Let the children design danger logos and create posters and charts about electricity. A safety display can be created.

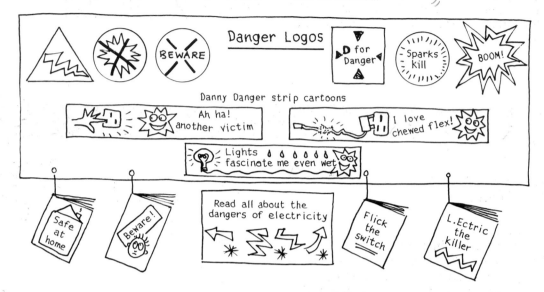

Area of study 2	P of S 1a	**ELECTRICAL CIRCUITS**	C71

Purpose

To demonstrate that a complete circuit is necessary for electrical appliances to work.

Materials needed

Covered wire suitable for electrical circuit making, wire cutters, a lamp and lamp-holder, a cuboid battery of the same voltage as the lamp, press-on terminals, a buzzer, balsa wood, drawing pins, paper clip.

Activity 1: Creating a circuit

Connect the lamp to the battery. Point out to the children some of the important words and ideas, including the fact that terminals need to be clean, the wire clean and bare at the connections (i.e. uninsulated), and that a good contact must be maintained at all connections. When the circuit is complete, the lamp lights up. Show the children what happens if you disconnect the circuit at any point.

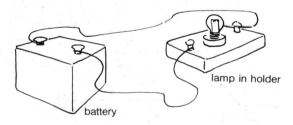

lamp in holder

battery

Activity 2: A buzzer circuit

Connect the lamp to the battery as in Activity 1. Take an additional piece of wire and put a buzzer into the circuit. Show the children what happens when the circuit is broken.

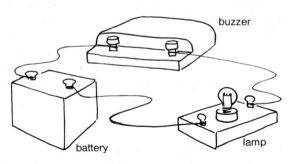

buzzer

battery

lamp

Activity 3: Switches

Ask the children what happens in a light circuit when you operate the switch. Make a switch as shown. Put the switch into a circuit similar to the one created in Activity 2. Let the children have a go!

A home-made switch

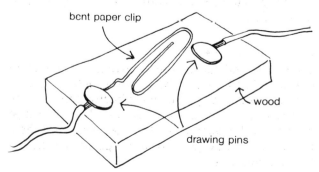

bent paper clip

wood

drawing pins

Activity 4: Fuses

A fuse in a circuit is a safety device to stop too much power entering and breaking equipment. If the maximum current for the fuse is exceeded the fuse blows breaking the circuit. Show the children the kind of fuse found in the fuse box at home, and take apart a disconnected electric plug to show them the fuse in it. Fuses can vary according to the maximum current they can carry. Tell the children that they should ON NO ACCOUNT touch the fuses or tamper with plugs at home.

Create a display of all the things used in the demonstration circuits, and then let the children handle them.

Copymaster 71 can be used to check that the children understand the necessity for a complete circuit for a flow of electricity.

 Area of study 3 | **P of S 1a**

GOOD AND BAD CONDUCTORS

 C72

Purpose
To show that some materials are good conductors of electricity and others are not.

Materials needed
Circuit making materials, including wire, wire cutters, lamp in holder, compatible battery, press-on terminals, crocodile clips and a variety of materials to try in the circuit such as a pencil, a necklace, a cereal packet or other cardboard box, a potato, glass, plastic, pottery, keys, a shoe (in fact any inanimate object to which crocodile clips can be attached).

Activity 1: Good/bad conductors
Make up a circuit including the battery and the lamp and attach crocodile clips to the free ends of the wire, as shown.

Let the children have a try at completing the circuit by connecting in a variety of materials in turn. Those that are good conductors will permit a current to pass

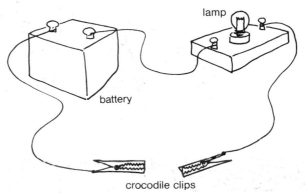

lamp

battery

crocodile clips

which will be sufficient to light the lamp. Poor conductors may light the lamp very dimly, and many materials will appear to be bad conductors.

The children can record this investigation on copymaster 72.

Area of study 4 | **P of S 2c**

ENERGY-PROVIDING FUELS

Purpose
To identify many of the fuels which provide energy.

Materials needed
Publicity materials and books about coal, oil, gas, nuclear fuels.

Activity 1: Fossil fuels
Investigate and discuss the formation and extraction of coal, oil and gas and the uses to which these fuels are put. Create a display using publicity materials, the children's projects, models, e.g. an oil rig, and tape recorded interviews with, for example, the school caretaker, the local garage owner, a gas-fitter or central heating engineer.

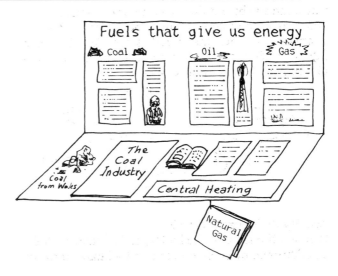

Fuels that give us energy

Coal   Oil   Gas

The Coal Industry

Coal from Wales

Central Heating

Natural Gas

Activity 2: Nuclear fuel
Explain the principle behind the production of nuclear fuels. This is quite difficult with children who may not have met sub-atomic particles. Tell them that nuclear reactors release energy by splitting uranium atoms (nuclear fission).

| Area of study 5 | P of S 3b | **FORCE AND MOVEMENT** | C73, 74 |

Purpose
To demonstrate that when things start to move or stop moving, forces are acting on them.

Materials needed
A bicycle with good brakes, toys with wheels, ramps; paper of several kinds (including tissue, copy, typing and cartridge paper) for making paper aeroplanes.

Activity 1: 'Start and stop' play with cars
Let the children establish as many ways as they can of starting and stopping the motion of a simple toy car. They will find they can start it moving by pushing it or putting it on a ramp, and it can be stopped by obstruction or using an 'escape road' with a soft surface such as sand. Encourage them to vary the force applied by asking: Does the car travel further if you push harder? Are there other things we can do to make it travel further?

The children can record their activities on copymaster 73.

Activity 2: 'Start' play with paper aeroplanes
Make some paper aeroplanes. There are several books currently available to help you with a simple design.

By playing with the aeroplanes, the children should identify important factors in flight: size and direction of force applied, and size, shape and material used in construction.

The children can follow the instructions on copymaster 74 and make their own aeroplanes.

Activity 3: Stopping force
Let the children examine and draw the working of bicycle brakes. The brake pads are pressed with force onto the bike rims. Get them to check what happens when only a little force is applied to the brakes, and to find out why using just front brakes is not a good idea. This work can be tied in with cycle safety by predicting what happens if the brake pads are worn.

| Area of study 6 | P of S 3b | **FORCE AND CHANGE IN SHAPE** |

Purpose
To show that when things are changed in shape forces are acting on them.

Materials needed
Modelling clay or Plasticine®, lightweight paper suitable for folding.

Activity 1: The use of force in clay modelling
If children squeeze or stretch out the clay in the course of modelling it, they can see that they are changing its shape by the application of pressure (force).

Activity 2: Paper folding
This is to show that the force applied to bring about change need not be great. Obtain a book on origami and try a number of paper folding exercises. In folding a force is applied. The paper adopts a new shape.

LIGHT CAN CHANGE DIRECTION

Purpose
To show that light can change direction.

Materials needed
A collection of reflective surfaces including, e.g. mirrors, lids from take-away meal packs, drinks; glass blocks, prisms, beakers of water.
Mirrors, spoons, pans, plain glass and black paper, a tank of water, polished metal; pictures of reflective surfaces including modern buildings, windscreens.

Activity 1: Play with sunlight
Let the children try reflecting sunlight off a wrist-watch, a mirror, the surface of a drink and other reflective surfaces onto the wall or ceiling. The light clearly changes direction in going from the reflective surface up to the ceiling. They can also play with glass blocks, prisms and glass beakers filled with water, or a beam of sunlight from a chink in a drawn curtain or blind. In these cases the light changes direction as it passes through the material, and when passed through a prism will give a rainbow effect. This is because white light is broken down into its constituent colours.

Set up a display of things that the children have played with.

Activity 2: Looking for reflections
Let the children look for as many surfaces as possible which allow reflections. Make a display including all

they find, and pictures of reflective surfaces which cannot be brought into the classroom such as modern buildings, puddles and windscreens. Include stories which use reflections in the plot, e.g. *The Ugly Duckling, Chicken Licken* and *Through the Looking Glass*. Discuss the differences in the sizes and shapes of the images they see, and the fact that images are sometimes inverted.

Copymaster 75 can be used to record work on images.

Activity 3: Refraction in water
Show the children a glass or transparent plastic beaker with some water in it. Put a pencil into the water. If they look carefully the pencil seems to 'bend' at the water surface. This is because the water makes the light (by which we see the pencil) change direction. Let the children try dipping other objects into the water.

LOOKING

Purpose
To explain that we see things when light scattered off objects reaches our eyes.

Materials needed
A darkroom, stock cupboard or other completely dark place; colour filters.

Activity 1: Can you see?
Take children into a totally darkened room. They will be unable to see anything. Put on the light or open the curtains and they will see everything. We need light for sight.

Activity 2: Colour filters
If the children view their surroundings through these they will see that everything takes on the hue of the filter. Tell the children that this is because light is being 'bounced' off everything in many directions, including through the filter and into their eyes.

Area of study 9	P of S 4d	

LIGHT TRAVELS IN STRAIGHT LINES ▶

Purpose
To show that light travels in straight lines.

Materials needed
String, pin, pieces of card; chalk, metre stick; torch, cotton, Blu-Tack®, block, paper and pins.

Activity 1: Corner trick
Ask two children to hold either end of a piece of string. Holding the string taut, and looking along the string, let one child take his/her end round a corner of the school building, so that he/she is out of sight. Clearly

light does not travel round right angle corners or we should be able to see round them. Ask the unseen child to move slowly towards the corner, holding the string taut all the while. Shout when the child comes just in sight. The string should be a straight line.

Activity 2: Pin-hole trick
Make two small holes in each of a number of pieces of card. Make the holes in the same place and the same distance apart on each card.

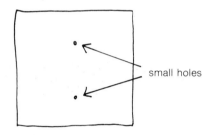

small holes

Thread all the cards onto a long piece of string, putting string through the lower hole in each card. Get a child to hold each end of the string, and then station children, one holding each card flat along the length of the string. Ask a child to look along the string through the furthest hole. Then have each pin-hole card put up in turn so that the viewer can see through each one (as below). When they are all up it will be seen that the string, which replicates the viewing line, is straight.

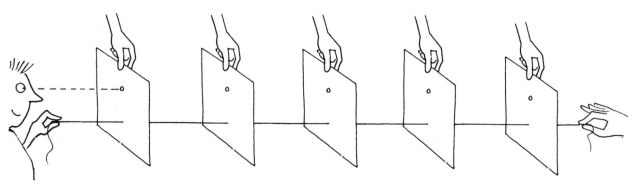

Activity 3: Shadows
If we look at shadows on the playground they are shorter when the Sun is high in the sky and longer when the Sun is lower. If we imagine a straight line drawn from the Sun to touch the edge of our body outline and then pass beyond us onto the ground, it falls at the edge of our shadow. Try out the idea of shadow length being related to the Sun's elevation by letting the children measure shadows in the same spot at different times of day. (Look also at Area of Study 14 *The Sun's inclination in the sky*.)

76

Activity 4: Shadow prediction
Stick some lengths of cotton onto the rim of a torch (as yet not switched on). Fix the torch on a block as shown.

Place a cardboard silhouette near the torch and fix it so that it stands up. Stick the strands of string to the rim of the silhouette with Blu-Tack® and then take each thread on to a sheet of paper and pin it there so that the cotton has made a straight line from the torch to the paper. From the positions of the pins predict where the shadow will come and draw it in. Switch on the torch.

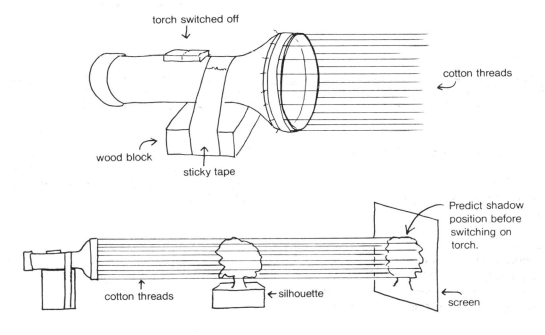

torch switched off

cotton threads

wood block

sticky tape

cotton threads ← silhouette

Predict shadow position before switching on torch.

screen

| Area of study 10 | P of S 4a | **EARS** |

Purpose
To show that we hear when sound reaches our ears and that ears are delicate and need care.

Materials needed
Earmuffs; books and pictures of different animals, showing their ears; information about looking after our ears and introductory books about what it means to be deaf.

Activity 1: We need ears to hear
Ask a child to wear the earmuffs and stand with his/her back to you, several paces away. Whisper a sentence. Get him/her to take off the earmuffs and repeat what they heard. It is unlikely they heard it all. Now get them to stand in the same position without the earmuffs, and whisper another sentence. They should hear it and be able to repeat it.

Activity 2: Outer ear shape and size
Explain that what we can see of our ears is the outer ear, and the part which does the work is inside our heads. Our outer ears collect sound, but are not terribly efficient, for they cannot move. Let the children name and find out about animals which have outer ears that they can move in the direction of the sound (e.g. cats, dogs and rabbits).

Activity 3: Care of ears
Discuss with the children that their ears are delicate instruments, that they should be kept clean but that they should NEVER put anything into their ears. Explain the dangers of repeated loud noise, of shouting down people's ears or smacking their ears.

Begin to discuss how deaf people communicate. Make sure the children understand that deaf people are just the same as hearing people, apart from in one respect, and they should not be treated as though they are silly.

Create a display of pictures of animal ears, ear care and 'sounds we like'.

| Area of study 11 | P of S 4a | **SOUND TRAVELS THROUGH MATERIALS** |

Purpose
To show that sound travels through materials other than air.

Materials needed
A solid wooden door, a long piece of wood 5 cm × 10 cm and about 2 m long, pieces of soft cloth, rubber bands

and a clock with an audible tick; tin cans, a nail, a hammer, string and large beads; a kitchen roll tube; polystyrene tiles, or other material suitable for sound-proofing, craft glue and a large shoe box; a plastic bag, a see-through tank filled with water.

Activity 1: Sound travels through wood (1)
Ask a pair of children to stand either side of a door. If one child stands with his/her ear to the door, the other should be able to whisper a message through the door, if they have their lips close to it.

Activity 2: Sound travels through wood (2)
Tie pieces of soft cloth onto the ends of a long piece of wood. Let one child put one end of the cloth-clad wood to his/her ear. Place the clock so that it touches the other end of the wood. The tick can be heard through the wood.

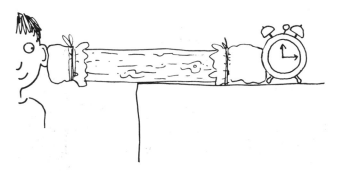

Activity 3: Sound travels through string
Puncture the ends of two empty cans using the hammer and nail, and push the ends of a long piece of string through. Tie off the string with a bead at the end to prevent the knot pulling through. Two children can use this like a telephone, by pulling the string taut and whispering to one another. They can experiment to

find out whether it works best with a string of any particular length.

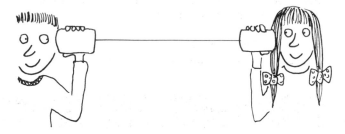

Activity 4: Sound travels through us!
Using a kitchen roll tube pressed gently against the chest, a little to the left of the middle, the children can listen to each other's heartbeat through the ribcage. If it proves too faint, ask the child whose heartbeat is to be heard to run up and down on the spot for a couple of minutes. Then listen.

Activity 5: Sound travels through water
Put a clock with a loud tick in a waterproof plastic bag. Lower the clock into a tank of water. The children should be able to hear the ticking by pressing their ears to the tank.

Activity 6: What does 'sound-proof' mean?
Explain to the children that when we want to keep out noise we can put a layer of something which is not very good at letting sound travel through it, all around a room. This is done in recording studios, and sometimes between the floors of blocks of flats. Try 'sound proofing' a shoe box with polystyrene (take care: if cut with a heat cutter, polystyrene gives off toxic fumes) or cotton wadding. Put a clock with an audible tick into the box and close the lid. The tick should be noticeably quieter.

Area of study 12	P of S 4d	REFLECTING SOUND

Purpose
To learn that sound can be reflected.

Materials needed
Paper, sticky tape, card, a clock or watch; books about bats and echo-sounding.

Activity 1: Listening for echoes
The school buildings may be placed so that you can stand between them and hear an echo when you shout. Alternatively, there may be a railway arch, subway or similar construction near the school where the children can hear echoes of their own voices. Explain to them that when we hear an echo, sound is 'bouncing back' to us, and the fact that the echo happens after we speak shows that sound takes time to travel.

Activity 2: Reflecting sound
Make two long cylinders from paper or thin card. Place them at angles to a large piece of stiff card held upright. Put a ticking clock or watch near one of the cylinders at the open end. Let a child put their ear to the other. The ticking will be heard quite clearly, for it has been reflected off the card.

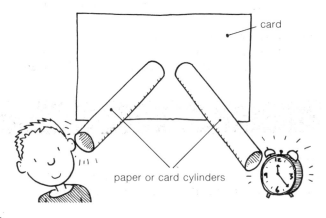

card

paper or card cylinders

Activity 3: Bats and echoes
Let the children find out how bats manage to catch insect prey on the wing, in almost total darkness, without bumping into anything.

Activity 4: Echo-sounding
The search for shoals of fish, sunken boats or submarines, treasure and even the Loch Ness monster involves sending sound waves to the river, lake or sea bed. Special equipment records the time taken for the echo to be received and thus the depth of water, and whether there is anything under the water surface or on the river, lake or sea bed.

Area of study 13	P of S 5b,c

MOON PHASES

 C76

Purpose
To observe and record the shape changes the Moon appears to undergo throughout the month.

Materials needed
Clear skies. Books about the Moon, paper and card, a projector and screen and a ball, an orrery.

Activity 1: The Moon's appearance
This work is best done in the second half of the autumn term. When the clocks go back, nightfall occurs before the children's bedtime, but after school has finished. Before you start this work you will need to ask parents if their children may do this work at home. You can say that it will only involve a few minutes once a week. When you have parental permission, then ask the children to look at the night sky on the next Monday night.

If they can see the Moon they can record its shape on their record sheet, copymaster 76. If they cannot see the Moon, then they should look out every evening that week until they spot it. Then the following week they should do the same and draw what they see. When they have made a drawing (if possible) in each of four consecutive weeks, they can bring their work back to school for discussion.

Activity 2: Moon facts
Ask the children to consult the reference sources about the Moon. Each new discovery can be recorded on a strip of paper and the children can then collate the facts under headings they devise themselves. In fact, with a little help from you they can create their own display.

Activity 3: Moon simulation
Take a small piece of card and trim it to fit a slide frame. Poke a pencil through the card to produce a circular hole. Use a slide projector to project a circular pool of light. Darken the room. Then if you pass a ball through the light it will appear to change shape just as the Moon does in its phases.

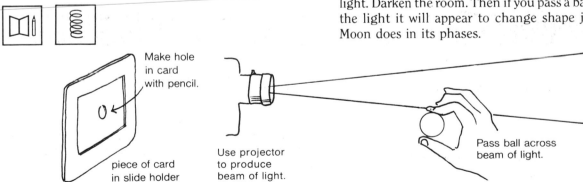

Make hole in card with pencil.

piece of card in slide holder

Use projector to produce beam of light.

Pass ball across beam of light.

Activity 4: Eclipses of the Moon
Explain to the children that an eclipse of the Moon happens when the Earth passes between the Moon and the Sun so that the Moon's orbit is in the Earth's shadow. Show the children how this can happen using an orrery.

Area of study 14	P of S 5c

THE SUN'S INCLINATION IN THE SKY

 C77

Purpose
To find out that the Sun's inclination in the sky changes from one part of the year to another.

Materials needed
Protective eyeshade for viewing the Sun. (Ask the school doctor what is suitable to shield the eyes from

the Sun. Do not use sun-glasses. The exposed ends of a developed roll of photographic film may be appropriate.) Prepared display board with stick-on Sun, or pen for drawing on the window.

Activity 1: Sun's position in the sky

Twice in the school year, perhaps around the longest and shortest days (June and December) set aside a week or so in which this experiment can be done. On the first sunny day in each of these periods, get each child in turn to don protective eye gear and observe the position of the Sun in the sky at 11.30 a.m. or thereabouts. If the Sun shines directly into the classroom, its position can be marked on a strategic window. If not, prepare a display board with the view of the skyline from the school, and the children can transfer their observations as stick-on Suns on the board. A comparison of the results at both times of year should show that the Sun is higher in the sky at 11.30 a.m. in the summer than it is in the winter.

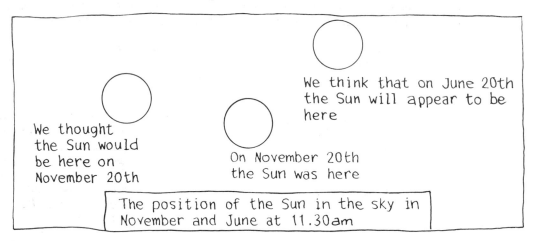

We thought the Sun would be here on November 20th

On November 20th the Sun was here

We think that on June 20th the Sun will appear to be here

The position of the Sun in the sky in November and June at 11.30am

Activity 2: Shadows

For two periods in the year, which may be one week or two depending on the weather pattern in your area, watch out for the first sunny day. Then at a time you have pre-set to fit your timetable (but somewhere around the middle of the day) get the children to go into the playground in pairs. On a spot they can remember and identify, ask them to draw around each other's shadow. They can measure and record the 'heights' of their shadows. Experimental results should show that the shadows are shorter in the summer months when the Sun is higher in the sky. To fully understand this work the children need to have mastered Area of Study 9, *Light travels in straight lines*.

The children can record their results on copymaster 77.

If a classroom display is mounted, several Suns can be placed on the board at different heights in the sky. If a thread is then pinned taut from each Sun over the little figure set on the ground, the children can see how the length of the 'shadow' behind the figure varies with the inclination of the Sun.

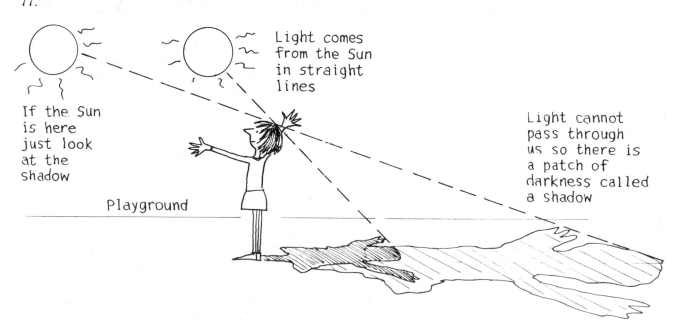

Light comes from the Sun in straight lines

If the Sun is here just look at the shadow

Light cannot pass through us so there is a patch of darkness called a shadow

Playground

Attainment target 4: Physical processes

Level 4	**Statements of attainment**	**Statements of attainment**

Statements of attainment

Pupils should:

a) be able to construct circuits containing a number of components in which switches are used to control electrical effects.

b) understand that an energy transfer is needed to make things work.

c) know that more than one force can act on an object and that forces can act in different directions.

d) know that light travels faster than sound.

e) be able to explain day and night, day length and year length in terms of the movements of the Earth around the Sun.

Statements of attainment

Pupils could:

design and make a circuit, for a working model which includes a number of bulbs or a motor or buzzer, and is controlled by switches.

explain that energy transfer is involved in the working of a clockwork toy, a steam engine and a battery-powered car.

use diagrams to show the direction of forces on objects and explain that the upward and downward forces are in balance when an object floats.

explain why, when viewed from a distance, a bat is heard to strike a ball after the impact is seen.

use a globe and lamp to model the Earth and Sun in order to explain how the relative positions of the two bodies and the rotation of the Earth about its axis give rise to day and night and determine length of day.

Area of study 1	P of S 1a	**CIRCUIT CONSTRUCTION**	C78

Purpose
To be able to make an electrical circuit.

Materials needed
Quantities of wire suitable for circuit-making, wire cutters, a variety of batteries; lamps in lamp-holders, buzzers and switches (or materials for making these, including wood blocks, drawing pins, paper clips or metal strips); press-on terminals and crocodile clips.

Activity 1: Rules of circuit-making
Remind the children of the need for clean terminals, bare wire at connections, good connections, a compatibility of power source and appliance and the need for a complete circuit without breaks. Make up a circuit containing a battery and lamp. Disconnect this circuit and give the children a chance to make their own circuit.

Activity 2: Buzzers and switches
Provide the children with a wide variety of circuit-making equipment and let them experiment in finding circuits that work.

Activity 3: Circuits in model-making
Let the children make shoe-box models such as a shop, room, disco or football stadium. They can then create a circuit for lighting it appropriately.

They can record their efforts on copymaster 78.

The models will make a stunning impact at a parents' evening display.

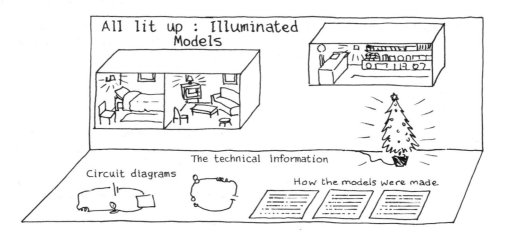

All lit up : Illuminated Models

The technical information

Circuit diagrams

How the models were made

<table>
<tr><td>Area of study
2</td><td>P of S
1a</td><td></td></tr>
</table>

MORSE

C79

Purpose
To explain that Morse employs electrical circuits and to send and interpret Morse messages.

Materials needed
Reference information about Morse, including a Morse alphabet; wire suitable for circuit-making, wire cutters, batteries and lamps, switches.

Activity 1: Morse messages
Let the children create a circuit with a power source, lamp and switch in it. Using the switch they can send a short Morse message to a friend, who can then use the equipment to reply.

Copymaster 79 can be used to record this experiment.

<table>
<tr><td>Area of study
3</td><td>P of S
2e</td><td></td></tr>
</table>

WHAT MAKES IT GO?

C80
—82

Purpose
To demonstrate that toys, machines and we ourselves need an energy source to work.

Materials needed
Simple toy cars, clockwork toys, battery operated toys; access to machines available in school, including tape recorder, television, clock, calculator and other machines in classroom use.

Activity 1: What makes toys 'go'?
Consult the work children have done at Level 2. Ask the children to bring in toys which move. The resulting collection should include the following:

● Simple toy cars
● Clockwork toys such as wind up cars, figures that walk or play a drum and water toys with paddles
● Cars and other vehicles which have flywheels
● Electrically operated toys such as battery operated robots, cars and tumbling clowns (using dry cells) and trains (using mains electricity).

Let the children try to work out what makes the toys 'go', while taking care to operate them gently.

Discuss with the children the idea that each toy has stored energy. When it starts to move the energy is converted into movement (kinetic) energy. In technical terms the stored energy may be strain energy contained in a spring, mechanical energy in a flywheel or

Toys that move

Clockwork   Flywheel   Battery

chemical energy converted into electrical energy in a battery.

Give the children copymaster 80 to record this work.

Activity 2: What makes machines work?
Make a survey of machines in the classroom, trying to include a wide range. Ask the children to say what it is that makes them 'go'. You could include, for example, a television and computer (electrical energy), some calculators (electrical energy converted from the chemical energy in the cell), a wind-up clock (strain energy in the spring), a rotary pencil sharpener (kinetic energy from human muscle power, converted from the chemical energy in the food we eat).

The children can record their understanding of power sources in machines on copymaster 81.

Activity 3: A home-made moving toy
Make a rubber band powered toy, as shown in Level 5 Area of Study 9, *Movement and forces*.

There is strain energy stored in the stretched rubber band which, when released, converts to kinetic energy. Copymaster 82 can be used to consolidate or test the children's learning.

| Area of study 4 | P of S 2e | # POWER SOURCES, ENERGY TRANSFER |

Purpose
To use power sources and devices which transfer energy.

Materials needed
A bicycle with gears and good brakes, a bottle opener, window catch, clawhammer, pincers, an old hand-sewing machine, junk modelling materials, including round cheese boxes and corrugated cardboard, rubber bands, Lego Technic® sets with a motor and drive belts.

Activity 1: Models with motors
Using Lego Technic®, let the children produce a model worked by a motor. If models with other power sources are available to you, e.g. model steam engines, then these should be shown and demonstrated to the children.

Activity 2: Bicycle gears
Gears speed things up or slow them down. Look carefully at the gears on the bike with the children. Suspend the bike so that the rear wheel and pedals will turn. Make a mark on the cogwheel which is attached to the pedals and a mark on the smaller cog round which the chain also goes. Get the children to count how many times the smaller cog goes round when the larger one goes round once. Then check how far round the larger cog goes when the smaller cogwheel makes one revolution. If you change gear on the bike, what difference does it make?

Activity 3: Gears at home
Show the children some tools we use at home which have gears, including, for example, an egg-beater and a mechanical drill. Let them compare the number of revolutions the smaller cog makes for each of the larger cog, and, if possible, the number of teeth the cogs have.

Activity 4: Making gears
To show what they do, gears should be attached to a working model. However, to show cogs at work, the children can make a large cog by sticking a strip of corrugated cardboard on the outside edge of a circular cheese box. Carefully give the cog an axle and attach it to a baseboard so that it will turn. Now fix so that the treads interlock a much smaller cog made from a similar, but smaller container. If one cog is turned the other will also turn. The children can also see what happens when they reverse the direction of turn. It is also worth experimenting with other potential resources such as metal bottle tops which already have a corrugated edge. Toys such as spirographs demonstrate the principle of cogs.

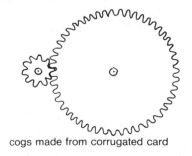

cogs made from corrugated card

Activity 5: Belts
Show the children appliances which transfer energy by means of a belt, e.g. a sewing machine, spinning wheel. Belts can be seen operating in many industrial and agricultural museums. The belts were often put on the machines with a twist in them so that the wear on the

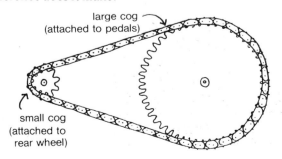

large cog
(attached to pedals)

small cog
(attached to rear wheel)

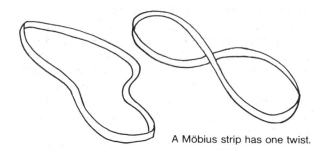

A Möbius strip has one twist.

belt was even. This idea can be tied in with Möbius strips.

Children can make their own Möbius strips from paper, and models with belts using, e.g. Lego Technic®.

Activity 6: Everyday levers
Show the children that we use levers a good deal, in using things such as a bottle opener, window catch, clawhammer and pincers.

GRAVITATIONAL FORCE AND WEIGHT
C83, 84

Purpose
To explain that falling objects are subject to a force of attraction towards the centre of the earth; that it is the effect of gravity on mass which gives objects weight; and that we measure the force of weight in newtons.

Materials needed
Pictures of astronauts in space capsules and on the Moon, video of astronauts moving in spacecraft; a collection of objects which you may drop safely from a height, including sticks and wood blocks, pebbles and leaves, bits of plastic, paper and card; a stairwell or window two floors up from which to drop these objects and a timer appropriate for this activity (see note in Activity 2); string, weights, clamps, protractors, second timers.

Activity 1: Gravitational force
Children know that if they drop something it falls to the ground, and if they jump, they come down again. Tell them that there is a force pulling things on the Earth towards its centre and this is called gravitational force. Because the force affects everything, the weight of things is a combined measure of mass and gravitational force and is measured in newtons. The children can speculate about what would happen if gravitational force was reduced. Show the children film of space travel.

Activity 2: What happens when we drop things
This activity needs careful setting up and supervision by a teacher. The things do need to be dropped from a height, and it will depend on your school where the most appropriate place is. If you are using a stairwell,

the well will have to be guarded so that no one enters it while the experiment is in progress. Similarly the ground below a high window will need a 'no-go' barrier to minimise danger to anyone underneath. The children can then drop a collection of objects. They can determine what factors influence the speed, motion and direction of fall. These will include shape and size.

Finding an appropriate timer for this task with children at this Level is a problem. Galileo used his own pulse: it may be possible to try this with the children.

Copymaster 83 can be used to record results of dropping experiments done by the children.

Activity 3: Pendula investigations
Let the children set up a pendulum by hanging a small weight from a length of string and suspending it from a clamp. They can time the 'swing', and determine how many swings there are to a minute. Ask them to guess what might happen if the length of the pendulum, the weight on it or the starting arc are changed. Let the children test out their ideas.

Results can be recorded on copymaster 84.

FORCES
C85

Purpose
To learn that objects can be acted on by more than one force, and that forces can act in different directions.

Materials needed
A water tank or deep bowl, a collection of objects which can be put into water without them being harmed, including, for example, corks, wood blocks,

plastic tubing, crockery, coins, metal bar or ruler, pebbles, fabric, card, paper; fishing floats and weights; plastic bottles, drinks cans, sandwich box, fabric pieces, modelling dough; some things with a low centre of gravity, such as wide-based vases, a ship's decanter, wobbly man and some with a high centre of gravity, such as a stem vase, a table lamp with a flexible stand; a pinball toy, video of part of a snooker game.

Activity 1: Finding a set of things that float

Let the children predict from a collection of objects which are those most likely to float. They can give reasons for their thinking. They can then test out their predictions, by putting all the objects in turn into a tank of water. Tell the children that the water appears to be 'holding up' the floating items, and is in fact exerting pressure or force on them. If the density of the object exceeds the density of water then the upthrust is not sufficient to hold it up.

The understanding that water exerts upward pressure and that this is evident in floating objects is important but difficult. The principle is: if the density of the object is greater than that of water, the object will sink despite the upward pressure. If the density of the object is less than that of water, it will displace its own weight of water and then float. The upthrust then equals the weight of the object. Even objects that sink appear to lose weight in water, owing to the upthrust.

Activity 2: To show upthrust

Try this out before doing it with children. Tie a piece of cotton thread to a large stone and try to lift the stone. Take care! The cotton will break. Tie another piece of cotton onto the stone. Place the stone and thread carefully in water. It should be possible to lift the stone in the water using the thread. You can relate this to the children's experience when swimming, i.e. the sense of weightlessness together with the ease with which they can move other swimmers away from them.

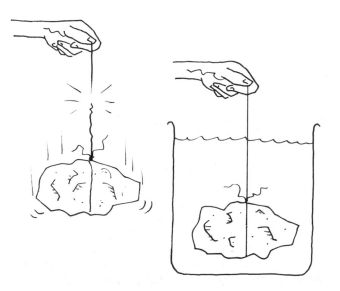

Activity 3: How fishing floats work

Show the children a range of fishing floats. Point out that the fisherman wants to be able to detect a 'bite' by means of the float, so the position it occupies in the water is very important. The weights on some floats are detachable and can be exchanged according to the depth at which you wish them to float. Other kinds of floats have the weights pinched onto the line beneath them and again you can vary the depth of the float in the water by using more or less shot. Make a collection of available floats and weights and the children can see how the weights affect the total density and the amount of float submerged.

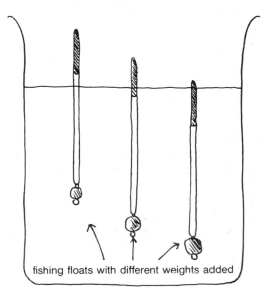

fishing floats with different weights added

Activity 4: Air-filled things and floating

The children can try putting items such as a plastic fizzy drink bottle with cap on, a drinks can, a sandwich box with lid, a piece of fabric with holes between the fibres such as wool and a small canoe made of modelling dough into the tank. With air in them they will float. When waterlogged or filled with water they will sink. The combination of the material the object is made from and the air is less dense than water. When the material is filled with water, the density exceeds that of water.

The children can record the results of sinking and floating experiments on copymaster 85.

Activity 5: Do floating and sinking rules apply to other liquids?

Carefully place an egg into fresh water. It will sink. Add some salt to the water and the egg will float. Ask the children what they can now say about river water compared with sea water.

Ask the children to try to guess what might happen to boats put into the water. Put small model boats into fresh and salt water samples. What can the children say about how the boats sit in the water? Discuss the idea of Plimsoll lines painted on boats to show the safe load in different waters.

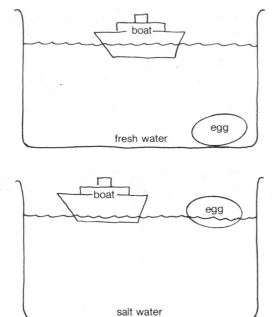

fresh water

salt water

Activity 6: Effect of change in forces on people
To start to understand the idea of balanced forces, talk about what happens when the children are sitting in a car or bus going along at a steady speed. If the vehicle turns or speeds up/slows down suddenly, what happens to them? Can they feel the effect of a change in the forces operating? Tell the children about the principle behind the discussion.

Activity 7: Centre of gravity
Explain to the children that things that are very stable have a low centre of gravity (balance point of the forces upon it). Show them a flower vase with a wide base or a ship's decanter, and a toy that always rights itself. Compare these with a tall vase with narrow stem or top-heavy vase, and a lamp with a flexible stand which will tip over if the lamp head is moved over too far. Discuss the relative stability of, for example, double-decker buses which have a low centre of gravity.

Just for fun let the children cut out the shape of the UK in card. Can they determine the 'centre' and which town lies nearest the centre of the UK?

Activity 8: Pinball and snooker
Let the children play with a pinball toy (or a simple game of marbles) and track the routes taken by the balls or marbles.

Watch a video of part of a snooker game, and 'pause' the film each time a ball changes direction, to discuss the direction of the forces on it and the direction of movement. The children can draw some diagrams while the film is held on 'pause'. Top-class players can cause the ball to swerve by making it spin, so some changes of direction for the white (cue) ball will have to be discussed in terms of collision and rotation.

Area of study	P of S	
7	3a	**STRUCTURE STRENGTH**

Purpose
To investigate some of the problems in bridge construction.

Materials needed
Metal Meccano®, books about bridges, pictures of bridges, balsa wood and planks of other kinds including e.g. plywood and hardboard, card, art straws, toy vehicles, a spring balance, two kitchen balances.

Activity 1: Bridges: shapes
Invite the children to build a variety of shapes using struts and nuts and bolts of Meccano®. If they bolt them tightly, they should find they can still push a square out of shape but not a triangle. If they examine pictures of real bridges, the kinds of shapes in common use can be discussed. They can test out paper bridges made with flat, square folded and triangular folded paper. If a piece of card is laid across, these can be made to carry a toy truck with increasingly heavy load, until the bridge fails.

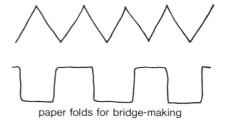

paper folds for bridge-making

Activity 2: Bridges: materials, size and thickness
If the children try out plank bridges of various materials, sizes and thicknesses, and push the same heavy toy vehicle across, the amount of sag can be measured by making a mark on a record sheet attached to the wall behind the plank.

Activity 3: Bridges: load variation
If a plank is laid with each end resting squarely on single pan scales and a heavy toy is pushed across, the children can detect the point(s) at which there is

maximum load, and think about the implications for bridge construction.

Activity 4: Bridges: testing design and construction
The children can make a variety of bridges, inventing truss and girder configurations, and test them to destruction, by adding weights to a spring balance attached to the centre point. Breakage should occur at weakest points and this knowledge will aid new designs.

Activity 5: Other structures
In addition to, or instead of, an investigation into bridges, the children can look at the same principles in the construction of towers, windmills and cranes.

EFFECTS OF FRICTION

Purpose
To describe the effects of friction.

Materials needed
A pencil rubber, water, cooking oil, a smooth surface; a block of wood, various materials to change the surface of a table, e.g. waxed paper, fabric, sheet plastic, sandpaper, string, masses.

Activity 1
Discuss what the children understand by friction, and how we experience it every day in, for example, moving about, stopping distance on a bicycle or in a vehicle, using matches and playing stringed instruments.

Activity 2: Vehicle tyres and friction
Replicate tyres by using an old pencil rubber, pressing it along a dry, wet and oily surface.

Activity 3: Friction investigation
Put a wood block with a string and a mass in a bag attached to it onto a variety of surfaces. Allow the string and bag to hang over a table edge. Add masses to the bag until the block starts to move.

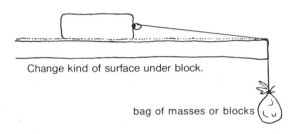

Change kind of surface under block.

bag of masses or blocks

The mass necessary to start the block moving on each of the surfaces can be recorded on copymaster 86.

Discuss with the children the effects of the surface on the mass necessary to start the block moving.

SPEED OF LIGHT AND SOUND

Purpose
To show that sound takes time to travel.

Materials needed
A cricket match, a drum.

Activity 1: Thunder and lightning
Remind the children that in a thunderstorm we can see the lightning before we hear the thunder even though they are happening at the same time. The sound of the flash takes longer to reach us than the sight of it. In fact if you count in seconds between the flash and the first roll of thunder you can tell approximately how far away the thunder and lightning occurred: five seconds means it is one mile away.

Activity 2: Cricket and sound on the playing field
If the children watch a cricket game they will *see* the batsman strike the ball before they *hear* the sound of it. You can test out this observation if you have a long enough playing field at school. On a calm day, try standing a child with a drum and drumstick at one end. If the remaining children stand at the other end, they may just detect a time lag between seeing a single beat on the drum and hearing it. It takes about one second for sound to travel 330 m.

Let the children record this experiment in cartoon form on copymaster 87.

Activity 3: Speed data
Tell the children that sound travels at about 1 070 feet per second (330 m per second) and light travels at 186 000 miles per second (that is 300 000 000 m per second). Compare this with other speed information like the fastest aircraft or land animals. Some aircraft travel faster than sound (that is through the sound barrier).

WHY NIGHT OCCURS

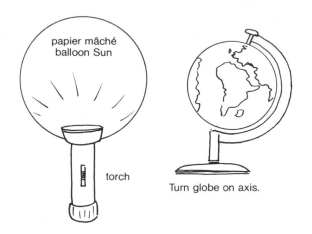

papier mâché balloon Sun

torch

Turn globe on axis.

Purpose
To explain why we have night-time.

Materials needed
Powerful torch, lampshade with orange cloth or tissue to cover, classroom globe; card sheets and string to make sandwich-boards, a map of the world (to copy), felt tips.

Activity 1: Day and night
Discuss with the children what daylight is and what night is. They may be able to say that our light comes from the Sun, that when there is no sunlight we are in darkness and this is what we call night. The problem then is to show why the Sun does not always give us light.

Explain that the reason we have day and night is that the world spins on its axis while the Sun remains still. Darken the room. Place a lit torch inside a covered lampshade to represent the Sun. Use a classroom globe or a balloon to represent the earth and, holding it some short distance away from, but on a level with the 'Sun', turn it on a north–south axis. The children can then see that part of the 'Earth' is lit by the 'Sun' while part remains in darkness. As the 'Earth' moves on its axis the part that was in darkness moves into the light, while the part that was formerly light moves into darkness.

Activity 2: The rotating Earth
Make four placards or sandwich-boards which children can wear on their backs. Draw a quarter of the world map on each one so that together they form a flat picture of the world (see illustration below). Make one plain orange sandwich-board to represent the Sun, and get the child wearing this to hold a lamp or torch. If the children wearing the world sandwich-boards stand in a circle close together and link hands or arms, they can walk round in a circle to represent the turning of the Earth on its axis. The 'Sun' child can shine the torch on the moving Earth and the children will see that only part of the Earth gets the Sun's light at any one time.

LENGTH OF THE DAY

C88

Purpose
To show that day length changes throughout the year.

Materials
Newspaper reports of times of sunrise and sunset at the time of year in which the work is done.

Activity 1: Sunrise and sunset
The children can note whether they had breakfast in daylight or darkness and at what time that was during one week in November and during one week in July. On those same days they could note the time the lights went on in their home in the evening.

The children's knowledge about nightfall and daylight can be recorded on copymaster 88. Following their winter-time recording the copymaster needs to be filed for use in the summer term. For those children who are unable to record these details or the times the Sun came up and went down, you can show them on their copymaster the times of nightfall and sunrise, using the times recorded in the newspaper as your own resource.

MEASURING TIME USING THE SUN

Purpose
To show that time used to be and can still be measured using the Sun.

Materials needed
Sunshine! Protective eye gear for observing the Sun, chalk, a stick and a chair, stiff card, protractors and scissors.

Activity 1: The Sun's position and time of day
Set aside a period of time for doing this work, when the Sun shines. Get the children to observe and record the position of the Sun in the sky at 9.15 a.m., 11.30 a.m., 1.30 p.m. and 3.15 p.m. (or at four other times which are better suited to your school work programme).

The children's record can be done on copymaster 89, or a class display can be made (see illustration below).

On the next sunny day the children may be able to estimate the time of day by consulting the Sun instead of a clock.

Activity 2: Shadow sticks
Push a stick, e.g. a broomstick, into the ground outside, away from buildings. Let the children mark and comment on the length and position of the stick's shadow at four times of day (say 9.30 a.m., 11.30 a.m., 1.30 p.m. and 3.30 p.m.). Let the children predict the length and position of the shadow in relation to the stick and draw it on paper. They can check their predictions by going and looking at the stick and its shadow. The next sunny day they can look first at the stick and its shadow and predict what the time is.

The children can do a similar investigation using a chair in the playground, or the shadow cast by the school building itself.

Activity 3: Sundials
Look at sundials. There may be one in a nearby garden.

The local garden centre may bring some along for you to see, or the children may be allowed to visit the garden centre. The children need to draw a variety of designs and styles of sundials which will show them that sundials have been used across the ages. Rubbings can be made and the materials from which sundials are made can be studied.

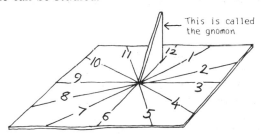

This is called the gnomon

Give the children some stiff card and a protractor and scissors and ask them to create a sundial. They will need to create a pointer which is a right-angled triangle with an angle of inclination the same as the latitude of your location, and to calibrate the dial by 'setting' it in exactly the same position every time they take it out to use: i.e. with the long side of the triangle pointing towards the north.

The children can record what their own sundial looks like, in addition to some of the designs they have seen on other sundials, on copymaster 90.

Activity 4: Telling the time by the Sun
On a day when you are sure the Sun is going to shine (!) remove or cover the clock and collect the children's watches. Give them to the headteacher for safe keeping. At a time that you have decided upon, say 11.10 a.m., ask the children to record what they think the exact time is by using their sundial.

When the children have completed their recording on copymaster 91 tell them what the exact time was.

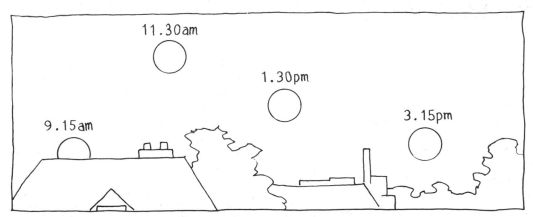

11.30am

1.30pm

9.15am

3.15pm

Class display: The Sun's position and time of day

OUR EARTH IN RELATION TO THE SUN

Purpose
To revise and extend a knowledge of the movement of the Earth about the Sun.

Materials needed
A globe and a torch, reference books about the planets, especially the Earth, information about time zones.

Activity 1: Earth year
The experiment which showed day and night (Area of Study 10 *Why night occurs,* page 88) can be repeated, and this time as well as rotating the globe on its axis it can be moved around the Sun to demonstrate the time we call a year.

Activity 2: Time zones
Because of the rotation of the Earth the time is different in different parts of the world. Some major banks and large hotels have clocks showing times around the world. If it is not possible to show these to the children you can arrange an array of clocks in the classroom to show time in different time zones across the world. You will need to find out where the time zones fall.

The children can decide on a moment when they are going to record time across the world on copy-master 92.

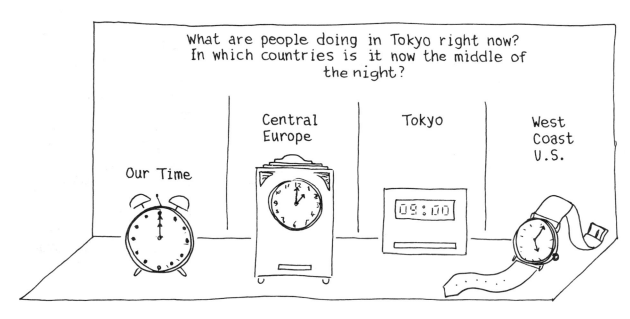

What are people doing in Tokyo right now?
In which countries is it now the middle of the night?

Central Europe

Tokyo

West Coast U.S.

Our Time

Attainment target 4: Physical processes

Statements of attainment	Statements of attainment
Pupils should:	Pupils could:
a) know how switches, relays, variable resistors, sensors and logic gates can be used to solve simple problems.	*devise circuits which switch on a bulb or buzzer when conditions change, for example hot-cold, light-dark, door open-door closed.*
b) understand that energy is transferred in any process and recognise transfers in a range of devices.	*identify the energy transfers involved in using a solar cell to drive a small motor, boiling water in an electric kettle, ringing a door bell, and pedalling a bicycle.*
c) understand the difference between renewable and non-renewable energy resources and the need for fuel economy.	*explain why it is necessary to avoid wastage of energy resources such as gas and oil which will not be naturally replenished.*
d) know that the size and direction of the resultant force on an object affects its movement.	*use diagrams to show the forces acting on a free-fall parachutist at different stages in descent.*
e) understand how the reflection of light enables objects to be seen.	*explain that when light strikes an object some of it is reflected and travels to the eye.*
f) know that sound is produced by a vibrating object and travels as a wave.	*explain how a range of sound sources, such as the voice, stringed instruments and loudspeakers, have vibrating parts and how sound travels by setting the air into vibration.*
g) be able to describe the motion of planets in the solar system.	*draw diagrams showing orbits of the planets and indicate the time it takes each planet to complete its orbit.*

Area of study 1	P of S 1b		C93, 94

CIRCUIT CONSTRUCTION

Purpose
To connect power sources and equipment in series and parallel, to draw these circuits using symbols, and observe and explain the outcomes.

Materials needed
Booklets that come with electrical appliances, wire for circuit-making, several batteries of the same size and strength, several lamps in holders compatible with the batteries, press-on terminals, crocodile clips, bells, resistors, ammeters and voltmeters.

Activity 1: Circuit symbols
If the children have not met them already, give them some of the commonly used symbols in circuit-making (see page 93). Let them look for circuit diagrams in booklets that come with electrical appliances such as radios and record players. They can see which circuit symbols they can interpret.

Copymaster 93 comprises a list of symbols.

Activity 2: Circuits in series: more batteries
The children should be familiar enough with circuits in series to be able to make a simple circuit of lamp and power source and then add other batteries in series. If you have an ammeter, introduce this into the circuit and the children can measure the current.

Activity 3: Circuits in series: more lamps
Add lamps in series to a simple lamp and power source circuit. The children should note that each additional lamp makes all the lamps become dimmer.

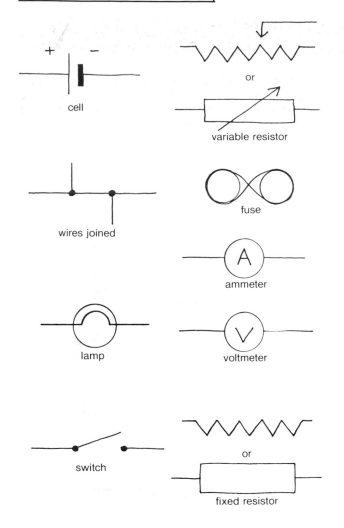

cell

variable resistor

wires joined

fuse

ammeter

lamp

voltmeter

switch

fixed resistor

Activity 4: Circuits in parallel: more batteries

Ask the children if they can add more batteries to a simple lamp and power source circuit, so that the lamp does not look brighter, but all batteries are contributing to light the lamp. They should connect the batteries in parallel. An ammeter will show the current in the circuit. They should find the current constant and the lamp of constant brightness however many batteries are in the circuit.

Activity 5: Circuits in parallel: more lamps

If the children now put more lamps in parallel, each lamp should be dimmer, because the battery power is shared.

All these experiments can be recorded on a worksheet such as copymaster 94, though the children may need more than one copy.

Activity 6: Designing a circuit

Ask the children to design a circuit, and then get a friend to make it up using the circuit diagram. They can see if their friend can do it without help, and whether the circuit does what was intended.

Activity 7: Wiring

At Level 4 the children may have had the opportunity to put a lighting circuit into a model. They could try this again from model and circuit design, through to completed project.

| Area of study 2 | P of S 1b | **VARYING THE FLOW OF ELECTRICITY** | C95, 96 |

Purpose

To vary the flow of electricity in circuits and note the effects.

Materials needed

Radio, simple electric model railway with controller, leaflets and booklets about household lighting switches and controllers, a rheostat (variable resistor), battery, compatible bulbs in bulb holders, switches, circuit wire, wire cutters, fuses and fuse wire.

Activity 1: Variable resistors in everyday life

Put the radio on and demonstrate the use of the volume control. To reduce the level of sound, the control offers more resistance to the current. 'Resistance' is how well a material resists electricity flowing through it.) See if the children can think of other controls which operate like this.

Dimmer switches for lighting operate in the same way, as do the controls in some cars which dim the lights on the instrument panel.

Activity 2: Model railway controller

Set up a simple loop of track and set the train going. Use the controller to vary the speed of the train. Let the children time how long the train takes to go round the track 10 times, with the controller set at various positions. Start the timing after the train has started moving at an even speed.

The children can record their results on copymaster 95.

Activity 3: Inserting a variable resistor in a circuit

Let the children construct a simple circuit with a battery, switch and bulb. Put a variable resistor, of the rheostat type, into the circuit. Move the control on the resistor and observe the brightness of the light bulb. Discuss with the children the length of resistance wire the current is passing through when the control is in various positions. Look at samples of fuse wire and compare the thicknesses with the maximum current that can be carried.

This experiment can be recorded on copymaster 96.

Area of study	P of S
3	**1e**

SWITCHES AND RELAYS

Purpose
To demonstrate how to use switches and relays in simple circuits.

'Make and break' s
switches children need
could attempt to make them
bolts, flexible metal strips, etc.

Materials needed
Batteries, bulbs, thin copper wire (obtainable from old transformers), paper clips, drawing pins, plastic covered wire, examples of commercial switches and relays, flexible metal strips (smooth), metal clips, large nails, electric bells/buzzers, bimetallic strip, electronic sensors.

Activity 1: Switches
Give the children a collection of materials such as flexible metal strips, drawing pins, paper clips, etc. and invite them to design and make two kinds of switches:

a) switches that go on or off when released,
b) switches that slide on/off and remain in position.

Test for ease of use, durability, overall construction and ease of connection in a simple circuit.

The children can draw the kinds of switches they produce on copymaster 97.

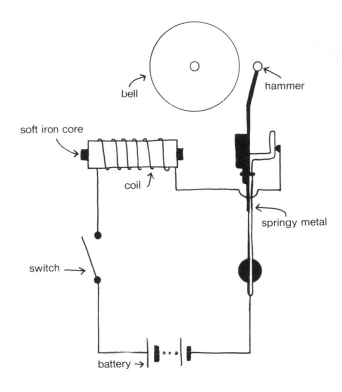

Activity 2: Electromagnets
Get the children to make a simple electromagnet by winding thin copper wire round a large nail and connecting the ends of the wire to a battery and a switch to complete a circuit. You will need to experiment to find out how many times the wire needs to be wound round to create an electromagnet.

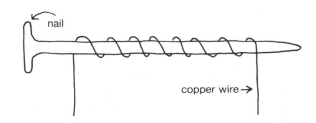

Try picking up small metallic objects. Release them by using the switch. Discuss where such devices might be useful, e.g. picking up cars or scrap metal, and then examine electric bells and buzzers.

Electric bells and buzzers work through the use of electromagnets which are rapidly switched on and off by the movement of the flexible arm which makes and breaks the electrical contact (see diagram opposite).

Activity 3: Bimetallic strips and thermostats
Demonstrate the effect of applying heat to a bimetallic strip. These strips are formed by the bonding together of two metals which have different expansion rates. Heat will cause the strip to bend as one metal expands more rapidly than the other. Get children to collect data about the existence of temperature controllers (thermostats) in their homes. Examples can be found in kettles, fires, irons and central heating controllers.

Copymaster 98 can be used to record information about thermostats at home.

Activity 4: Sensors
If you have light sensors or other sensors available try out some simple detection circuits with the children. Ask the children to seek out the use of sensors in everyday life, e.g. shop-lifting detector barriers, burglar and fire alarms, counting devices and sound sensitive devices. Make a group list of all the items that the children discover.

LOGIC GATES

Purpose
To explain logic gates in decision-making and control circuits.

Materials needed
Circuit symbols, dice and counters.

Activity 1: Decisions
The children will be familiar with tables and decision-making trees from their work in Mathematics (AT5 Level 4). To understand logic gates it is useful to build on this knowledge by posing some 'dilemmas' which can be analysed in terms of the number of options open to them. For example, the answer to the question 'Can I go swimming?' might have two embedded questions:

a) Have I enough money?
b) Am I free at the right time?

If the answer to a) is NO then it is not possible to go even if the answer to b) is YES. All of the possible answers can be laid out in the form of a table.

Have I enough money?	Am I free at the right time?	Can I go swimming?
NO	NO	NO
YES	NO	NO
NO	YES	NO
YES	YES	YES

In only one case is it possible to go swimming, and that is where the answers to the questions are Yes to (a) **AND** Yes to (b). This is a **TRUTH TABLE** and is an example of an **AND** situation. In an **AND** gate it is necessary to have two inputs in order to get an output.

Give the children some examples of this sort of decision-making.

Another sort of truth table can be constructed in answer to a question such as 'Do I need to wear my fur-lined boots?' You will need your boots if it is cold or raining.

The table looks like this:

Is it cold?	Is it raining?	Do I need to wear my fur-lined boots?
NO	NO	NO
YES	NO	YES
NO	YES	YES
YES	YES	YES

There is only one possible occasion when you do *not* need your boots. In this case, the table is produced on the basis of whether one **OR** the other question is answered in the positive. With an **OR** gate either of the two inputs produces the output.

Give the children some examples of this sort of decision-making.

The final logic gate is a **NOT** gate. This is rather different from the other two in that it has only one input and it acts, apparently, rather strangely. If there is a positive input then there is no output. If there is no input there is an output.

Play the logic gates game on copymaster 99.

Activity 2: Logic gates in use
Try to get the children to consider examples of where they meet or hear about logic gates being used, e.g. frost warning devices, some burglar alarms, some car alarms, cameras with warnings for light levels and washing machines.

The children can try designing some simple circuits. For example, a simple car alarm which would sound if the door was opened would be an example of an **AND** circuit. A simplified diagram is shown here.

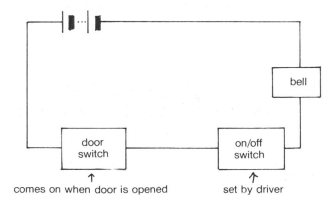

comes on when door is opened   set by driver

ENERGY IS ESSENTIAL

Purpose
To demonstrate that energy is essential to human beings in all they do and is essential to change in anything.

Activity 1: The need for energy
Discuss with the children some of the things they like doing, all the things they might do in a typical 24 hours, things which take a lot of energy and things

which take very little energy. Emphasise that we do not have to be energetic to use energy! We need it even when asleep.

Copymaster 100 gives children the chance to compare the amount of energy they need in a range of activities.

Activity 2: Energy sources at home and in school
Discuss with the children what energy sources are needed for us to run our lives as we do. Include, for example, heat, light and electricity, and the use of cars, television, washing machines, kettles. Let the children try to predict what we would do if an energy source was suddenly not there.

Copymaster 101 enables the children to record their speculations.

Activity 3: Energy and change
Discuss the idea that energy is behind all kinds of change and movement and therefore essential for anything to 'happen' in our universe.

ENERGY STORAGE AND TRANSFER
Area of study 6 | P of S 2e

Purpose
To discuss energy storage and transfer.

Materials needed
Pictures and sample objects which prompt a discussion about energy storage and transfer.

Activity 1: Energy transfer discussion
Assemble a number of pictures and items on which to base a discussion of energy storage and transfer. Here are some examples:

- Pictures of pleasure boats worked by paddles
- Walkie-talkies
- A saucepan with an egg boiling in water in it on an electric hot plate
- A solar-powered calculator
- A toy aircraft with rubber-band propeller.

With the children's help work out the energy storage and transfer links for each of your examples. The ones above present the following:

- Paddle-boat: Chemical energy in human muscle converted to kinetic energy forcing the paddle to move
- Walkie-talkie: Chemical energy in human body converts to kinetic energy in voice box and transmitted as vibrations to receiver, where it is converted to electrical energy (impulses), which are picked up by the listener in kinetic energy form (vibrations)
- Saucepan: Electrical energy in the hotplate converts to kinetic energy, causing the plate to heat. This transfer to the pan, the water and the egg, where it converts to chemical energy, 'cooking' the egg
- Calculator: Solar energy converted to electrical energy to enable the calculator to work
- Aircraft: Strain energy in the rubber-band converts to kinetic energy.

ENERGY RESOURCES
Area of study 7 | P of S 2d

Purpose
To find out about renewable and non-renewable energy resources.

Materials needed
Books, information packs and films about fossil fuels, nuclear power and alternative energy sources like water, wind and solar power.

Activity 1: Renewable and non-renewable resources
Remind the children of work they have done at Level 3 about fuels in the home. Explain that supplies of fossil fuels like coal and natural gas are finite and non-renewable (for they took many thousands, even millions of years to make). Help the children to identify other sources of energy which are infinite. These include water, wind and solar power.

Activity 2: Energy source investigation
Let the children choose one of our current main energy sources, for example oil, natural gas or nuclear power and look at the following:

- Locations of supplies (from a geographical and political point of view)
- Limitations on use because of location and size of supply
- Problems in recycling and waste disposal
- Environmental impact.

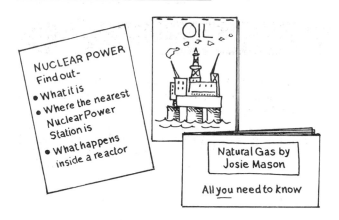

Activity 3: Tidal power
Investigate energy schemes to harness the tide in estuaries, for example the River Severn barrage scheme.

Activity 4: Wind power
Discuss efforts to redevelop wind power. There is a scheme afoot already in Cornwall where some wind machines have been erected. Research this with the children. Some farms have their own windmills.

Activity 5: Water power
Look at the working of a hydro-electric power station, particularly noting its location and the shape of the

dams constructed for efficient energy utilisation as well as strength of structure.

Activity 6: Testing for solar power
The children know the Sun's energy warms them, but to demonstrate this they could take the temperature of a bowl of water, leave it in a sunny place and take its temperature at half-hour intervals. Discuss the implications of this for solar heating.

If you have sensors available, let the children use the temperature sensor and take a series of readings throughout the day, close to the school building, on its sunny side and shady side. When compared they should demonstrate that the air near the building on the sunny side gets warmer than on the shady side. Discuss the implications of this for solar heating, and were it possible, where they should be placed in your school.

Activity 7: Solar panels
Find out if there are any suppliers of solar panels in the locality, and any buildings which have solar panels built in. Ask a representative to tell the children how the panels work, and visit and inspect solar-heated buildings.

Discuss the use of solar cells in some calculators and in satellites (for example weather satellites) orbiting earth.

Area of study 8	P of S 2c	**FUEL ECONOMY AND EFFICIENCY**

Purpose
To identify why and how fuels can be used economically and efficiently.

Materials needed
Booklets and books on home insulation and heat loss prevention, motor magazines, including *Motoring Which?* and car advertising materials.

Activity 1: Fuel economy at home
Look at ways of keeping homes warm by minimising heat loss. Include various ways of insulating roofs and walls and other factors such as window size, window 'fit' and double glazing. Mention also the timing of heating to match the family's needs and 'economy rates' for heating. Invite a representative from a

building firm which boasts of 'heat-saving homes' to discuss their methods. A member of local authority staff may help by telling the children (or perhaps the children could interview them in their office) about home insulation, and what grants are given for.

Activity 2: Cars and fuel economy
Compare a range of cars for fuel economy, using advertisements and test reports. Compare fuel economy with running costs for different cars. Discuss any conflict there may be between the car owner's wish for cheapness and efficiency. Interview a garage proprietor or local representative of a motoring organisation about fuels and fuel economy.

Arrange a display to combine the children's work on what to do to fuel homes and cars economically and efficiently.

MOVEMENT AND FORCES

Purpose
To show that how much an object moves depends on the size and direction of the forces on it.

Materials needed
Cotton reels, rubber-bands, spent matches, card, sticks (such as plant support sticks), beads, long pins with stout heads, balsa wood, craft knives, short nails and a hammer, a long balloon, a round balloon, nylon fishing line, plastic drinking straws, sticky tape, Lego®.

Activity 1: Rubber-band force: cotton reel toy
With a cotton reel, a rubber-band and two spent matches the children can make a rubber-band-powered toy. Reduce friction on one end of the cotton reel by rubbing it with a candle. Anchor the band at the other end of the cotton reel through the centre of the reel with a short length of matchstick. Push a longer matchstick into the rubber-band at the waxed side of the reel and twist until quite tight. Try out how many turns are necessary to make it move, not over- or under-winding. Make sure one end of the longer match extends beyond the rim of the reel, so that it touches the ground. Set down the reel and it should move. If you have difficulties it may help to have a smooth bead through which the rubber-band is passed at the driving end. Once the children have got their models moving effectively, they can experiment to see whether more turns of the band means the toy travels a greater distance. They can try and make it climb a ramp, too.

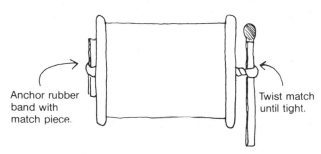

Anchor rubber band with match piece.

Twist match until tight.

Activity 2: Rubber-band force: paddle-boat
Let the children make a paddle-boat out of balsa wood, as shown below. (The paddle may be made from balsa wood or thick card.)

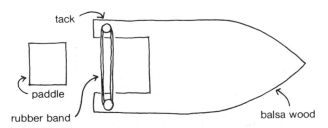

tack

paddle

rubber band

balsa wood

Let the children try out their boats in water. Can they predict what will happen if they wind the band the other way?

Copymaster 102 can be used for the children to record how they made their boats and how test 'sailings' went.

Activity 3: Wind force: windmill
Let the children make paper or thin card windmills as shown here.

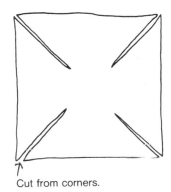 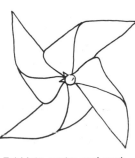

Cut from corners.

Fold into centre and push paper fastener through.

The details of this construction have been set out on copymaster 103 so that the children can make it for themselves.

Test out the windmills by blowing or applying wind from a hairdryer, to see whether the direction and force of the wind make a difference to the motion of the windmill.

Activity 4: Wind force: balloon rocket
Attach one end of a length of nylon fishing line at one side of the room. Blow up a long balloon and keep the air in it by putting a clothes peg on the open end. Stick a plastic drinking straw to the balloon lengthwise with sticky tape. Pass the free end of the line through the straw, and ask a child to hold the line so that it is just taut. Move the balloon so that it is near the child's hand. Stand clear of line. Countdown! Release the peg. The children should (when they stop laughing) be able to say what makes the rocket go. Let them experiment to see if the wind power will take the rocket up a sloping line.

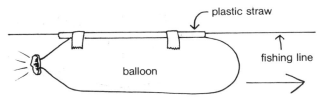

plastic straw

fishing line

balloon

Activity 5: Wind force: go-kart

Get the children to make a small Lego® trolley. Inflate a balloon and pinch the neck together with a peg,

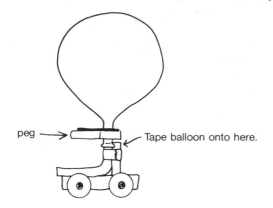

peg → Tape balloon onto here.

making sure that there is enough neck to grip. Fix this end over the end of a piece of bendy plastic straw and seal the balloon onto the straw with sticky tape. Stick the balloon to the kart with tape. Release the peg and away it should go! Ask the children what makes it go.

Activity 6: Hydraulics and pneumatics

Discuss the fact that liquids transmit pressure and that this is put to use in the brake systems of many cars, the 'tip-up' mechanisms in trucks and lorries and in mechanical diggers.

Pneumatic systems utilise compressed air or other gases. There are sophisticated construction sets available for children, like Lego® Technics which enable children to construct working models.

  STOPPING A MOVING OBJECT

Area of study 10 | P of S 3b | C104

Purpose

To demonstrate that the faster an object is moving, the greater the force/time needed to stop it.

Materials needed

Pictures of playground equipment, a baby's spinning top, a gyroscope, toy cars and a long wooden ramp, marbles and plastic track such as curtain track.

Activity 1: Stopping on playground equipment

Look at the pictures of playground equipment, which should include a roundabout, swings and bucking horse. Discuss the relative force or time needed to stop the equipment when it is moving slowly or fast.

Activity 2: Stopping a spinning top

If children play with the top they will see that the faster they make it go before releasing it, the longer it will go before stopping.

Activity 3: Stopping a gyroscope

Demonstrate with the gyroscope that the more turns you give to the string on it and the faster it goes, the longer it spins before stopping.

Activity 4: Speed and stopping distance using toy cars

Set up a long fixed ramp. Let the children put a toy car on it at a marked spot, half-way up the ramp, and mark where the car comes to rest. They can measure the distance travelled. They will need to do this a number of times, reject those where the car swerves, and take the average of the measured distances. They should

then put the same car at the top of the ramp, and, again, for a number of trials, measure the distance travelled. There is a link here between the speed achieved by the car and its stopping distance.

Activity 5: Speed and distance using marbles

As in Activity 4, let the children release a marble half-way up a fixed sloping track and record over several trials the distance the marble travels. The same marble can then be placed at the top of the same fixed track, and the distance travelled recorded again. The link between speed and distance travelled can be established.

Note that accurate timing over the distances measured in Activities 4 and 5 is difficult. Speed is related to time and the children should begin to understand that such a link exists. There is a timer investigation in Area of Study 11, from which you could select a timer to make for children to use at this Level.

Results of the distances travelled in the trials in Activities 4 or 5 can be recorded on copymaster 104.

Activity 6: Stopping distance and road safety

Ask the local police force if a road safety officer can come to talk to the children specifically about stopping distances (i.e. when the steady force of the brake is applied) and their implications for pedestrians, cyclists and everyone using the roads. Ask the police for some statistics about stopping distances and recreate these distances in the playground, getting the children to stand the appropriate distance apart.

FORCES, DISTANCE AND TIME

Purpose

To explain and to measure forces, distance and time.

Materials needed

A variety of springs and clamps, tins, a water supply, metal strips, a tool kit and vice, marbles, a wooden board, pieces of wood, wood glue, kit to make an electronic timer; long fixed ramp, balloon pump, rubber bands and string, balsa wood, a variety of toy cars and other vehicles, a newton meter; materials to make a trolley, string, masses and hanger, paper strips, washing-up liquid, paint.

Activity 1: Making timers

Set up as an open-ended investigation so that the children can explore ways of making timers suitable for measuring different lengths of time. For example, they can set up bouncing springs, water drip tins, vibrating metal strips, rolling ball timers, electronic timer kits.

Activity 2: Stopping force

Let the children set up a long ramp. Attach an inverted balloon pump to the end and fix a thin piece of balsa wood to that. Pull inner tube out of pump so that it lies ready for pushing. Put each of a variety of vehicles of different mass at the top of the ramp and allow them to bump the pump at the bottom. A chalk mark on the ramp where the pump started, and where it finished, for each vehicle will enable the children to record and talk about a link between mass and stopping force. The experiment can be repeated with vehicles of equal mass but different-sized wheels (Lego® can be used here).

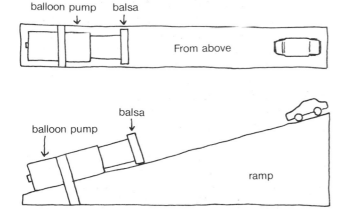

The results of this experiment can be recorded on copymaster 105.

Activity 3: Pulling force

Experiment with a newton meter to determine, for example, the force necessary to open different doors in school.

Activity 4: Stretching springs

Let the children carry this out themselves. Pin a piece of paper to a backing board or wall. Suspend a spring from a clamp in front of the paper. Mark the length of the spring on the paper. Suspend masses, one at a time, from the spring, and mark where the spring reaches.

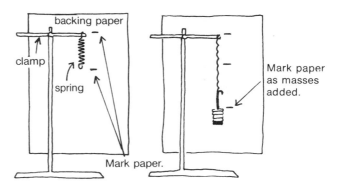

Results can be recorded on copymaster 106 and a graph can be drawn.

Activity 5: Distance and time link

Get the children to work in pairs. In the playground, mark a starting point, walk in a straight line for 10 seconds, and mark the point reached. Rest for 10 seconds and then walk back to the start, timing the journey. Measure the distance travelled. Do this experiment a number of times and draw a graph of average distance × time. The resulting graph should follow the shape shown.

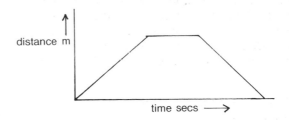

The results can be entered on copymaster 107 and a graph can be drawn.

Activity 6: Force and acceleration link

Construct a trolley from wood, Meccano® or Lego®. Attach a piece of string to the front end of the trolley and allow the string to run over the edge of a table. Attach a bag to the free end of the string. Now fix a strip of paper along the route to be taken by the trolley. Make a drip timer by piercing a hole in an empty can with a drawing pin. Set the trolley down on the strip of paper and tape the can on the back, so that the pin-

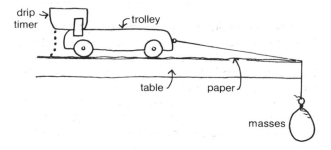

drip timer · trolley · table · paper · masses

hole is beyond the back of the trolley. Put the trolley at its starting point and add one mass to the bag, but get a child to support the bag until you say 'go'. Pour a little washing-up liquid to which powder paint has been added (paint is slightly more viscous than water) into the timer and let go of the bag. As the trolley runs the length of the table, the timer drips will mark the paper. Catch the trolley before it runs right off the table! Staunch the remaining drips from the timer with a cloth. Do the 'run' several times more, with different coloured liquids and more masses added to the bag.

From the marks on the paper, the children will be able to see that the trolley goes faster when more force is applied to it, for the faster the trolley moves, the fewer the drips.

Area of study 12 · P of S 4d,f · REFLECTION · C108

Purpose
To explain the basics of light reflection.

Materials needed
A slide projector and a slide card with a slit in it; a mirror, coloured filters.

Activity 1: Reflecting a light beam
Set up the slide projector with the slit card in place so that it shines a narrow beam of light just above a table. Advise the children of the proper use of the projector, for it can get hot. Let the children put a piece of paper onto the table, switch on the projector, and place the upended mirror in the path of the beam. If they swivel the mirror they will see that the light bounces off the mirror, but always at the same angle at which it struck the mirror.

Some of these angles can be drawn, using the light beam and mirror, on copymaster 108.

Activity 2: Effects of coloured filters
We see objects as coloured because the light 'bounced' off them to our eyes is red or blue or whatever, the other colours having been absorbed.

Using the same apparatus as in Activity 1, let the children look at the effects of shining the light beam through one or more filters. The filters absorb all but one colour, that of the resulting beam.

In daylight, the children can look through the filters and record what has happened to the colours of objects around the room.

Area of study 13 · P of S 4d,f · MIRRORS AND LENSES · C109

Purpose
To find out about mirrors and lenses.

Materials needed
Single flat mirrors, pencil beam torches, mirrors taped together down one edge, concave and convex mirrors; a tall carton, plane plastic mirrors, greaseproof paper, beads, torch or lamp; concave and convex lenses, a slide projector and a slide card with a slit in it.

Activity 1: Single mirror
Let the children take the initiative with a single mirror and see what they can find out about it. If they get stuck you will have to give them clues which may lead them to do some of the following things: draw half a picture and complete it with a reflected image; draw a picture with an axis of symmetry and put the mirror on the axis; play around with the mirror and pictures in books and comics, giving people two heads, etc; explore what happens to the beam of light from a pencil torch when it is shone at the mirror.

Some of their discoveries can be recorded on copymaster 109.

Activity 2: Two mirrors
The children can see what happens when two mirrors are put together. With two mirrors taped together along a short side, as shown, they can explore the images produced.

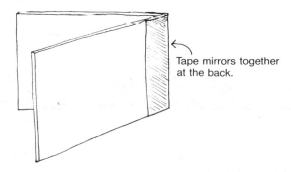

Tape mirrors together at the back.

100

Activity 3: Concave and convex mirrors

Let the children explore the images produced by these kinds of mirror and their uses.

Activity 4: Make a periscope

This way of making a periscope (and the kaleidoscope below) comes from Neil Ardley's 'My Science Book of Light'.

Show the children how to make a periscope, by fixing two plastic mirrors at the appropriate angles to one another within a carton or tall cardboard cuboid. You need an eye hole in the appropriate place to see one mirror, and an entry panel for light to reach the other mirror. These diagrams show how to make it.

Discuss with the children what is happening to enable us to see round corners, using reflected light.

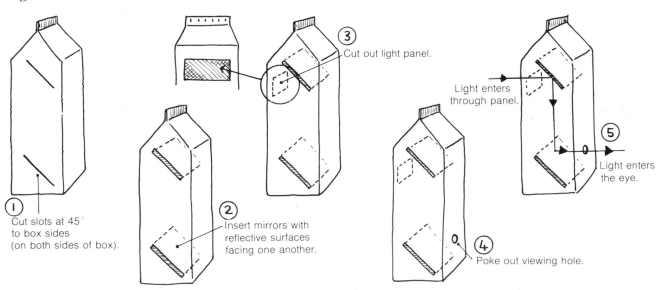

① Cut slots at 45° to box sides (on both sides of box).

② Insert mirrors with reflective surfaces facing one another.

③ Cut out light panel.

④ Poke out viewing hole.

⑤ Light enters the eye.

Light enters through panel.

Activity 5: Make a kaleidoscope

Tape together three rectangular mirrors all of the same size, along their longer sides. Stick greaseproof or other translucent paper over one end of the resulting prism. Cut a 'lid' to fit the other and make a small hole in the centre before sticking it down. Drop beads through the hole, and then look into the prism through the hole, while allowing a small lamp or torch to shine on the translucent end. The 'repeat' pattern is the result of multiple reflection. Here are some diagrams showing how it is made.

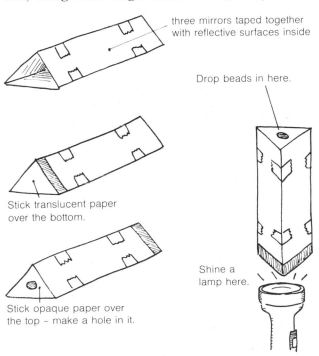

three mirrors taped together with reflective surfaces inside

Stick translucent paper over the bottom.

Stick opaque paper over the top – make a hole in it.

Drop beads in here.

Shine a lamp here.

Activity 6: Lenses

Let the children examine a variety of convex and concave lenses. Set up the slide projector with the slit card in place so that it shines a narrow beam of light. Let the children explore what happens when this beam is passed through each of the kinds of lenses. Discuss the use of lenses in magnifiers, spectacles, binoculars, telescopes and microscopes, and how magnification is achieved.

Activity 7: A visiting optician

Ask an optician or optical technician to come and talk to the children about what an eye test involves, how lenses can correct defects in vision and how a prescription for spectacles is made up.

| Area of study 14 | P of S 4b | **MUSICAL INSTRUMENTS** | C110 |

Purpose

To explain how musical sounds are produced in some musical instruments.

Materials needed

A collection of musical instruments including at least one percussion, one wind and one stringed instrument;

containers with fitting tops; dried pulses, rice and pasta to make shakers, jam jars, stout boxes, rubber bands, wooden blocks or rods, pieces of hard plastic and metal pipe, string.

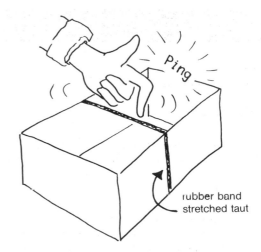

rubber band stretched taut

Activity 1: Looking at instruments

Look at and discuss with the children the shape and construction of a range of instruments. Include at least one percussion (e.g. drum, piano), one wind (e.g. clarinet, recorder), and one stringed instrument (e.g. violin, guitar). Listen to them being played on tape. If possible ask a child or teacher who plays each of the instruments to come and tell the children about the different parts, how it works, and show them how it is played.

Activity 2: Shakers

Make shakers by putting dried pulses, rice or pasta into jars with well-fitting lids. Add them to the percussion instruments.

Activity 3: String things

A really stout cardboard or plastic box will support a rubber band or string stretched tightly around it. The 'string' does need to be very taut. The children can try plucking or scraping the 'string'.

Activity 4: Things to bang

A row of jam jars with different amounts of coloured water in them sound melodic when tapped with a stick. Try tapping two wooden blocks together. Suspend pieces of wood, plastic pipe and metal pipe and try tapping those.

Create a music corner where the children can go and experiment quietly with a range of instruments and use junk materials to produce their own. Display pictures of instruments from other cultures and try to borrow some if they are available.

Copymaster 110 can be used for the children's pictures of instruments.

102

SOUND PRODUCTION

Purpose
To show that vibrating things produce sounds.

Materials needed
A stringed instrument, a home-made rubber-band instrument; a tuning fork; string and fishing lines of various thicknesses, nails, hammer, balsa wood, weights; natural history books; a drum or tambour, sand, a tuning fork.

Activity 1: Vibration in instruments
If you pluck the strings on a violin or guitar, the children will be able to see the movement of the string back and forth (vibration). They may also be able to feel the vibration by touching the body of the instrument. When they pluck the rubber band on a home-made 'band box' they may be able to see the vibration of the band. If a tapped tuning fork is placed on the forehead the vibration of the fork can be felt.

Tell the children that vibration occurs in all things that make a sound.

Activity 2: Voice-box vibration
If the children touch their own voice-box when they hum or speak they can feel the vibration. Using natural history books let the children investigate the voices and the production of sounds by a range of animals.

Activity 3: Loudspeakers and vibration
If the school has a stereo sound system with speakers, the children can gently put their hand on the speaker when there is sound coming through, and feel the vibration.

Activity 4: Effects of string thickness
If you have a guitar available, the children can look at the thickness of the strings, and pluck and scrape each

string in turn. They will notice that thicker strings produce lower notes. In addition to, or instead of a guitar, fix some strings and nylon fishing lines across a board or table as shown. Use a piece of balsa wood as a bridge in each case, and secure weights to the free end of the strings adding weights until the string is really taut. The children can pluck and scrape the strings and note the link between thickness and whether the note produced is low or high.

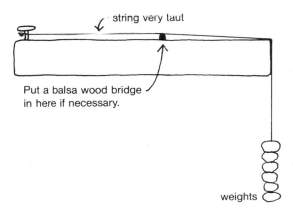

Activity 5: Sound makes things vibrate in a regular way
From their earlier activities the children will know that something vibrates to make sound. If you drop a little sand on the membrane of a tambour and stand a tuning fork that has been struck in the centre, the sand forms into concentric circles.

The children can record the results of this experiment pictorially on copymaster 111.

FREQUENCY, PITCH, AMPLITUDE

Purpose
To learn the meaning of frequency, pitch and amplitude.

Materials needed
Tuning forks of different pitch, an oscilloscope, microphone and tone generator.

Activity 1: Tuning forks
Let the children examine and strike the tuning forks. The forks may be marked with the note they make and the number of vibrations (often called cycles) per second. If they are unmarked tell the children that forks giving higher notes vibrate more quickly. For example:

middle C is 256 vibrations (cycles) per second
top C is 512 vibrations (cycles) per second.

Activity 2: A look at frequency
Borrow an oscilloscope from a secondary school and show the children what it does. They will be able to

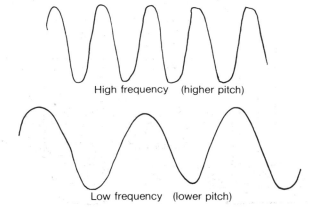

show, using their own voices, that frequency (as shown by the waves) changes according to how high or low the sound received is (i.e. its pitch).

Activity 3: A look at amplitude

Set up an oscilloscope and the other apparatus. Let the children try singing a note or playing a note on an instrument softly and loudly. Observe what happens to the waves on the oscilloscope. The extent of the 'peak' and 'trough' of the wave should increase as the note gets louder. We call this *amplitude*.

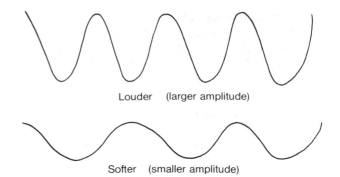

Louder   (larger amplitude)

Softer   (smaller amplitude)

 Area of study **17** P of S **4b**

HOW SOUND TRAVELS

Purpose

To explain how sound travels.

Materials needed

A slinky spring, a chair.

Activity 1

Get one child to hold one end of the spring on the floor, while another child stands on a chair and holds the other end of the spring aloft. A slight tweak to start a vibration at one end sets up a motion in the spring, where each turn of the spring seems to close up and move apart. Sound travels in waves with just this motion.

 Area of study **18** P of S **4c**

NOISE CONTROL

 C112, 113

Purpose

To understand that we can and should sometimes reduce noise or minimise its effects.

Materials needed

A Walkman®, industrial earmuffs, tape recorders.

Activity 1: Noise we make

Explain the dangers of having the volume control on a Walkman® turned up, and the nuisance it causes to other people (e.g. when on a bus or train). Discuss also the noise pollution that aircraft, cars and motor bikes can cause, and what we can do to effect change.

Copymaster 112 gives children the opportunity to write about noise that annoys. They can choose a local noise problem such as aircraft noise or write about noises they themselves hate.

Activity 2: Industrial noise
Discuss the necessity for some workers to take precautions against noise by wearing earmuffs, e.g. those on tractors or using road drills and in some factories.

Activity 3: Measuring noise levels
Using the experience the children may have had in AT2 Level 4 Area of Study 8, get them to design a noise investigation experiment and carry it out, using tape recorders. They may, for example, decide to record the noise at various events at school, e.g. in the playground, in the dining hall, in assembly. Alternatively they may wish to look at extraneous noise affecting them in school, e.g. roadworks, or heavy traffic.

Copymaster 113 presents a suggested framework for a noise investigation.

Area of study 19	P of S 5c	**THE SOLAR SYSTEM**

Purpose
To explain in basic terms the configuration of the planets in the solar system and their relative sizes.

Materials needed
A good reference book about the solar system, Plasticine® and pictures of the planets and space travel; trundle wheels and metre rules.

Activity 1: The scale of the solar system
If you give the children the data below and some centimetre squared paper or string they should be able to cut strips or pieces representing the diameters of the planets and the Sun. The children can display these to make comparison easy.

	Scaled data Diameter in centimetres	Scaled data Distance from Sun in metres
Sun	1000	
Mercury	3	.58
Venus	9	1.08
Earth	9	1.50
Mars	5	2.28
Jupiter	100	7.78
Saturn	90	14.27
Uranus	30	28.70
Neptune	30	44.97
Pluto	4	59.07

Take the children and some metre trundle wheels and rules outside and station a child to represent the Sun and then a child to represent each of the planets at the correct scale distance away from the 'Sun'.

Activity 2: Space exploration
Compile a dossier of pictures of planets and space travel. These can be the inspiration for groups of children to carry out further research, e.g. the efforts of man to explore space, what is now known about each of the planets. Search out any information which local museums and the museum service have about our solar system. A visit to a planetarium is a great treat! Write to an observatory and space centres for any schools packs they may produce.

Area of study 20	P of S 5b	**WHAT IS A STAR?**	C114, 115

Purpose
To give some information about stars.

Materials needed
Astronomy books, projector and 'card' slides; night sky charts.

Activity 1: Star facts
Let the children search the books for star facts, including the names and pictures of the constellations.

They can record star facts, including the ideas that stars do not have points and do give out light, on copymaster 114.

They can each draw the constellation of their own star sign on copymaster 115.

Activity 2: Constellations
Use the projector and slides made from card pieces cut to size. Get the children to draw star constellations on the card, and then to make a pin-hole through the middle of each star. Then when a card slide is put into the projector, the points of light on the screen will represent the pattern of the stars. This needs a little practice but can produce very effective representations.

Activity 3: Stargazing

If possible let the children view the sky after dark on some clear nights and identify some of the stars and any bright planets visible. Look in the newspapers for charts giving the location of stars and planets in the night sky at different times of the year.

Key Stage Two

Name _____ **Year/Class** _____

L e v e l 2	?							▦✓								
	🔍							📖✏								
	📏							💡								
L e v e l 3	**H**							📖✏								
	🔍							▂▃▄								
	⚖							🌀								
	⏱							I.2.3.4.								
	🥛															
L e v e l 4	?							¹₂₃↓								
	H							✓								
	⚖							📖✏								
	🔍							📈								
	⏱							🌀								
	🥛							📔								
L e v e l 5	?							🥛								
	🔍							A▸B								
	⏱															

Key Stage Two

Name _____

Year/Class _____

		Level 2 Comments	Level 3 Comments	Level 4 Comments	Level 5 Comments
AT 2	a				
	b				
	c				
AT 3	a				
	b				
	c				
AT 4	a				
	b				
	c				